# *Prayer*

JEREMY P. TARCHER/PENGUIN
*a member of Penguin Group (USA) Inc.*
*New York*

TITLES BY ERNEST HOLMES
Published by Tarcher/Penguin

*365 Science of Mind*
*The Art of Life*
*Creative Mind*
*Creative Mind and Success*
*The Essential Ernest Holmes*
*The Hidden Power of the Bible*
*Love and Law: The Unpublished Teachings*
*Prayer*
*The Science of Mind: The Definitive Edition*
*This Thing Called You*

JEREMY P. TARCHER/PENGUIN

*a member of Penguin Group (USA) Inc.*

*New York*

# *Prayer*

## How to Pray Effectively
### from *The Science of Mind*

# ERNEST HOLMES

JEREMY P. TARCHER/PENGUIN
Published by the Penguin Group
Penguin Group (USA) Inc., 375 Hudson Street, New York, New York 10014, USA · Penguin Group (Canada), 90
Eglinton Avenue East, Suite 700, Toronto, Ontario M4P 2Y3, Canada (a division of Pearson Penguin Canada Inc.) ·
Penguin Books Ltd, 80 Strand, London WC2R 0RL, England · Penguin Ireland, 25 St Stephen's Green, Dublin 2,
Ireland (a division of Penguin Books Ltd) · Penguin Group (Australia), 250 Camberwell Road, Camberwell, Victoria
3124, Australia (a division of Pearson Australia Group Pty Ltd) · Penguin Books India Pvt Ltd, 11 Community Centre,
Panchsheel Park, New Delhi–110 017, India · Penguin Group (NZ), 67 Apollo Drive, Rosedale, North Shore 0632,
New Zealand (a division of Pearson New Zealand Ltd) · Penguin Books (South Africa) (Pty) Ltd, 24 Sturdee Avenue,
Rosebank, Johannesburg 2196, South Africa

Penguin Books Ltd, Registered Offices:
80 Strand, London WC2R 0RL, England

First Jeremy P. Tarcher/Penguin edition 2008
Copyright © 2008 by United Church of Religious Science
Material originally published in *The Science of Mind* © 1938

Most Tarcher/Penguin books are available at special quantity discounts for bulk purchase for sales promotions,
premiums, fund-raising, and educational needs. Special books or book excerpts also can be created to fit specific
needs. For details, write Penguin Group (USA) Inc. Special Markets, 375 Hudson Street, New York, NY 10014.

Library of Congress Cataloging-in-Publication Data

Holmes, Ernest, 1887–1960.
Prayer : how to pray effectively from the science of mind / Ernest Holmes.
—1st Jeremy P. Tarcher/Penguin ed.
p. cm.
ISBN 978-1-58542-605-8
1. Prayer—United Church of Religious Science. 2. United Church of Religious Science—Doctrines.
3. New Thought. 4. Spiritual life—United Church of Religious Science.
I. Holmes, Ernest, 1887–1960. Science of mind. II. Title.
BP605.U53H645 2008 2007029920
299'.93—dc22

Printed in the United States of America
1 3 5 7 9 10 8 6 4 2

BOOK DESIGN BY NICOLE LAROCHE

# Contents

*Freedom from Sin—Free from the Sensitiveness—I Keep the Promise—Love
Gleams Through the Mist—No Bondage—No Condemnation—No False Habit—
No Hypnotism nor False Suggestion—No Mistakes—There Are No
Responsibilities—The Time Has Come—Within Thy Law Is Freedom*

*Beauty—Friendship of the Spirit and of Man—I Serve—I Shall Not Doubt
nor Fear—I Was Told to Live—Law—Love—Love Dissolves All Fear—
My Affairs—My Business—My Profession—No Delays—No Misrepresentations—
No Obstructions—No Over-Action nor Inaction—One with Perfect Action—
Peace, Poise and Power—Stillness and Receptivity—Thanksgiving and Praise—
The Inner Light—The Night Is Filled with Peace—The Seal of
Approval—The Secret Way—The Shining Path—The Things I Need
Come to Me—The Way Is Made Clear Before Me*

*As Love Enters, Fear Departs—Infinite Life Within—My Feet Shall Not
Falter—No Harm Shall Befall You—Power to Live—The Circle of Love—
The Circle of Protection—The Power Within Blesses All—The Quick
Answer—A Song of Joy—Born of Eternal Day—I Arise and Go Forth—
Inspiration—The Dawn Has Come*

*Complete Confidence—Drawing the Good—I Fear No Evil—I Have Known,
Always—I Meet My Good—My Atmosphere—My Good Is Complete—My Own
Shall Come to Me—My Soul Reflects Thy Life—Sorrow Flees from Me—
Substance and Supply—The Ever and the All—The House of Love*

*Arise, My Spirit—Command My Soul—Despair Gives Way to Joy—Free
Spirit Within Me—Fullness of Light—He Who Inhabits Eternity—I Listen—*

## *Foreword*
### The Reverend Joel Fotinos

*Most men who believe in God believe in prayer; but our idea of prayer changes as our idea of God changes; and it is natural for each to feel that his way of praying is the correct way. But we should bear in mind that the prayers which are effective—no matter whose prayers they may be—are effec*tive because they embody certain universal principles which, when understood, can be consciously used.

—ERNEST HOLMES

## HOLMES ON PRAYER

You are about to read a book that could change your life forever. I've taught classes on prayer for many years, and I've come to understand that most people believe two things about prayer: they think they are praying incorrectly, or worse, they feel they don't even know *how* to pray. And yet, prayer touches the lives of everyone who has ever wondered about a higher power, which means all of us.

Ernest Holmes took prayer very seriously. He meant prayer—specifically the form of affirmative prayer that he called spiritual mind treatment—to be a tool to live a better life. He had the startling and revolutionary belief that all prayers can be answered, as long as the person praying knew how to pray aright.

Answered prayers, Holmes wrote, are not based on begging, pleading, or good works. "Nothing could bring greater discouragement than to labor under the delusion that God is a Being of moods, who might answer *some* prayers and not others," he writes in this book. Instead, Holmes believed that there was a way of praying that would not only be answered, but also become a gateway to form a greater connection with the Divine. Prayer, in Holmes's philosophy, is not something that is mysterious and for only a rare few, but instead is something imminently practical for all who would seek how to pray correctly.

By demystifying what prayer is (and is not), Holmes makes prayer accessible and empowering: "Prayer is not an act of overcoming God's reluctance, but should be an *active* acceptance of His highest willingness. Through prayer we recognize a spiritual law, that has always existed, and put ourselves in alignment with it."

## WHAT THIS BOOK IS

Holmes wrote extensively about prayer and spiritual mind treatment in all of his books, most notably in his magnum opus, *The Science of Mind*, which is considered the "textbook" for the many students of his teachings. I've worked with many students who want to learn more about prayer but are intimidated by the sheer size of *The Science of Mind*'s nearly eight hundred pages, and have never discovered the sections on prayer found within. Worse, they don't find the pages and pages of beautiful meditations and affirmative treatments that are included in the latter half of the book.

*Prayer: How to Pray Effectively from* "The Science of Mind" highlights those writings about prayer—extracting them from the textbook and putting them squarely into the hands of the many who want to know not only how to pray, but how to pray so that their prayers are answered. This book does not replace Holmes's opus, but does serve as a good introduction to it, and I hope encourages each reader to continue studying the source text, and most importantly to maintain Holmes's principles in their lives.

## HOW TO USE THIS BOOK

Think of this book as an active "prayerbook"—a guide to prayer and also a book of prayers. In the first section you receive instruction about how to pray affirmatively. Read it, study it, add notes, apply it, and make it your own.

In the second section of this book, you will find dozens of beautiful, poetic, and transforming meditations and prayers on many different topics. I might suggest starting each day by reading from this book, so that you begin your morning aligning your thoughts from a very "high" place. Flip through the pages of meditations until you find the one (or ones) that you feel speak to your soul. Read it silently several times, then close your eyes and allow the words to go in deeply. Finally, read them aloud for there is power in speaking your words. During the day, return to the meditation several times so that the message of the words can resonate deeply.

"We need not *coerce,* we do not *create* the power, but we must LET this Great Power operate through us," Holmes reminds us. By repeated readings of these prayers, you will be able to let them become more true for you. As with anything, the more actively you apply this book in your life, the more results you will no doubt see— both within and without.

> Treatment is not *willing* things to happen; it is to provide within ourselves an avenue through which they may happen. Treatment opens up the avenues of thought, expands the consciousness, and lets Reality through; it clarifies the mentality, removes the obstruction of thought and lets in the Light; it removes doubt and fear, in the realization of the Presence of Spirit, and is necessary while we are confronted by obstructions or obstacles. We already live in a Perfect Universe, but It needs to be seen mentally before It can become a part of our experience.

# CHAPTER ONE

# The Power of Thought

## SPIRITUAL MIND HEALING

It has taken humanity thousands of years to learn that it has the power to control its own destiny. From the Bible we have the assurance: "As a man thinketh in his heart, so is he." The old Greek philosophers understood something of the meaning of thought. *What we expect*, said Aristotle, *that we find. What we wish*, said Demosthenes, *that we believe.* And Shakespeare is accredited with the saying: "There is nothing either good or bad but thinking makes it so." It is one thing to *know* a principle, another to *apply* it.

The modern commercial world accepts the slogan: "He can who *thinks* he can." Throughout the ages many persons have realized that causation is from within. True, the thousands of unhappy beings would indicate that a comparatively small number have used this knowledge for their benefit; yet the day for incredulous skepticism or shallow criticism of the power of thought has passed. Unless we discredit all human testimony, we are forced to the conclusion that bodily healing of all manner of sickness by mental and spiritual means, is a fact. Physicians of highest repute are assiduously betaking themselves to a serious study of mental phenomena and mental processes. They are realizing the incredible possibilities of dominion resident in the dynamic forces of the mental realm. A belief in and an acceptance of mental healing has arrived in the most orthodox of medical circles, and is being increasingly approved as a legitimate and useful healing agent.

## THE BASIS FOR MENTAL HEALING

M uch in this field is as yet obscure and imperfectly understood, for the scientific study of mind is still in its infancy; but the fact that a misuse of mental and spiritual laws is at the root of many unhappy conditions incident to the physical life, stands out clear and sharp.

The first principle fundamental to the understanding of the operation of thought is, that we are surrounded by an Infinite Intelligence. The possibility of healing physical disease, changing environment, attracting friends and demonstrating supply through the power of right thinking, rests entirely on the theory that we are surrounded by an Infinite Mind, which reacts to our thought according to Law.

We comprehend the meaning of Infinite Intelligence only in a small degree, but because we are spiritual beings, we do sense the presence of an Intelligence which is beyond human comprehension—an Intelligence which is great enough to encompass the past, to understand the present, and to be Father of the future. It is the Cause of everything that has been, and is that out of which must unfold everything that is to be. Our own intelligence is one of Its activities and is of like nature to It.

## THE ACT OF INCARNATION

At the level of our self-comprehension, we know and understand the nature of God. This self-knowing, which is God-knowing, has the possibility of an eternal expansion. As individual intelligence, we communicate with each other—are able to respond to each other—and in so doing we establish the fact that intelligence responds to intelligence. This same law must hold good, whether we think of finite intelligence responding to finite intelligence, or Infinite Intelligence responding to finite intelligence—*for intelligence is the same in ESSENCE wherever we find it*. We may conclude that Infinite Intelligence responds to us by the very necessity of being true to Its own Nature.

But how does It respond? It can respond only by corresponding, which means that the Infinite Intelligence responds to us by a direct impartation of Itself through us. "The highest God and the innermost God is One God." So with Jesus we may say: "The Father and I are One." Whatever intelligence we possess is some degree of the One Intelligence, which we call God.

The Infinite Mind, then, imparts Itself to the finite, through the act of incarnation. The progress of the human race is a result of that process whereby Intelligence passes, by successive degrees of incarnation, through evolution, into the human mind.

## ACTIVITY OF THE ONE MIND

We are living in an Intelligent Universe, which responds to our mental states. To the extent that we learn to control these mental states, we shall automatically control our environment. This is why we are studying *the power of thought* as we approach the subject of spiritual mind healing. This is what is meant by the practical application of this Science to the problems of everyday living. The result of this mental work is what is meant by demonstration.

In the great Universal Mind, man is a center of intelligence, and every time he thinks he sets Mind in action. Because of the Oneness of Mind, It cannot know anything outside Itself, and therefore cannot contradict any thought given It, but must reflect whatever is cast into It. We are immersed in an Infinite Creative Medium which, because of Its Nature, must create after the pattern our thought gives It. Jesus understood this, and in a few simple words laid down the law of life: "It is done unto you AS you believe." No more simple and yet no more profound statement could be made.

# IT IS DONE UNTO US

What a marvelous thought to bear in mind: that it is done unto us! We need not *coerce*, we do not *create* the power, but we must LET this Great Power operate through us.

In the Infinity of Mind, there is nothing but Mind and what Mind does—Its operations. *This Mind is acted upon by our thought, and in this way thought becomes the law of our lives.* It is just as much a law in our individual lives as God's thought is in the larger life of the Universe. WE DO NOT CREATE. WE USE THE POWER OF THE ONE MIND, WHICH CREATES FOR US! Our beliefs and our deep-seated convictions inevitably out-picture and reflect themselves in our experience and environment, both in the physical condition of the body, and in the larger world of our affairs. What we outwardly are, and what we are to become, *depends upon what we are thinking*, for this is the way we are using Creative Power. The sooner we release our minds from the thought that *we* have to create, the sooner we shall be able to work in line with Spirit. Always man *uses*; he never *creates* anything. The united intelligence of the human race could not make a single rosebud; but our thought, centered in Mind, is *using* the Creative Power of the Universe.

Law of Life is a law of thought—an activity of consciousness—the Power flows through us. The Spirit can do for us only what It can do through us. Unless we are able to provide the consciousness, It cannot make the gift. The Power behind all things is without limit, but in working for us It must work through us. Realizing, then, that while the Power is limitless, It must become operative through our own thought, we shall see that what we need is not some greater power, but a greater consciousness, a deeper realization of life, a more sublime concept of Being, a more intimate concept of an already indwelling God, *Who is personal to us by virtue of being personified through us.*

## THOUGHT FORCE

Thought force is a movement of consciousness in a field of mechanical but intelligent Law. The movement of consciousness upon itself creates a motion or vibration upon Substance, *the force of which is equal to the embodiment of the thought set in motion.* For everything that happens in the objective world, there must be something in the subjective world which perfectly balances it.

Let us suppose, for illustration, that the Universe is nothing but water, permeated by an Infinite Intelligence. Imagine that every time this Intelligence moves, or thinks, ice is formed in the water, exactly corresponding to the thought. We might have countless pieces of ice of different form, color, and size, but *these pieces of ice would still be water!* If we could heat the entire mass, it would melt, and all forms would again become fluid. Nothing would have changed except form. The physical universe is Spirit in form.

First is Intelligence; then the Word, the idea, the image, the concept; then the movement toward the thing. Thought is an actual working power. Otherwise, there would be nothing by which the Universe could be governed.

## THE ATMOSPHERE
## OF OUR THINKING

We are all immersed in the atmosphere of our own thinking, which is the direct result of all we have ever said, thought or done. This decides what is to take place in our lives. Thought attracts what is like itself and repels what is unlike. We are drawn toward those things which we mentally image. Most of the inner processes of our thought have been unconscious, but *when we understand the Law, we learn to consciously embody what we wish, and think of this only, and then we are drawn silently toward it.*

The emphasis on true mental healing is insistently on God, the One Mind, the One Soul, the One Being, ever-present and ever-available; and on man's ability and right to make himself receptive to this healing Presence—a realization of the essential divinity of our own nature, and the truth that no evil can live in this Presence. We must unify ourselves with the great Whole. The man who dares to fling his thought out into Universal Intelligence, with the assurance of one who realizes his divine nature and its relation to the Universe—and dares to claim all there is—will find an ever-creative good at hand to aid him. God will honor his request. To the soul that knows its own divinity, all else must gravitate. Let us, then, enlarge our thought processes, and dare to think in Universal terms. Let us dare to believe that every constructive word is invincible!

## INDUCING THOUGHT

That which thought has done, thought can un-do. Lifelong habits of wrong thinking can be consciously and deliberately neutralized, and an entirely new order of mental and emotional reaction established in Mind. Merely to abstain from wrong thinking is not enough; there must be active right thinking. We must become *actively* constructive and happy in our thinking—not merely *passively* so. New and wholesome ideas of life, vitality and hope must be accepted and incorporated into the sub-stratum of our mental life, so that a more wholesome externalization may manifest in our bodily condition and environment.

Since we must all begin right where we are, most of us will be compelled to begin our healing work with a mechanical process. We should take the highest thought we have, and attempt to enlarge on this consciousness until it embraces a more vital concept of Reality. Consciousness in this sense means an inner embodiment of ideas. If one wishes to demonstrate prosperity, he must first have a consciousness of prosperity; if he wishes health, he must embody the idea of health. This is more than faith; it is the knowledge that we are dealing with Law. While a certain consciousness may be mechanically induced, of course, the more spontaneity put into the mechanical word, the more power the word must have.

## CHOOSING THOUGHT

We cannot live a choiceless life. Every day, every moment, every second, there is choice. If it were not so we would not be individuals.

We have the right to choose what we wish to experience. We have the right to choose the kind of companions with whom we wish to associate; to say in what city and in what type of house we would like to live. We are individuals and the only way we can be individuals is to be spontaneous. There is no such thing as a mechanistic individuality, it must have the essential elements of spontaneity. There is no spontaneity and no individuality without prerogative. There can be no choice unless there is something from which to choose, otherwise the ability to choose would be merely a fantasy. Therefore, there must be not only the possibility of choice; but the liability of experiencing that which is chosen.

We have a right to choose what we shall induce in Mind. The *way* in which our thoughts are to become manifest, we cannot always see—nor should we be disturbed that we do not see the way—because effect is potential in cause. "I am Alpha and Omega," and all that comes between cause and effect. Cause and effect are really one, and if we have a given cause set in motion, the effect will have to equal the cause. One is the inside and the other the outside of the same thing. A certain, specific, intelligent idea in Mind, will produce a certain, specific, concrete manifestation equal to itself. There is One Infinite Principle, One Infinite Thought-Stuff, One Infinite Creative Power, but countless numbers of forms, which change as the specific idea behind them changes.

## THOUGHTS ARE THINGS

Health and sickness are largely externalizations of our dominant mental and spiritual states. An emotional shock, or a mind filled with thoughts of fear, has been known to cause the momentary stoppage or acceleration of the heart. Physicians now testify that, under emotional stress, particularly anger, the blood leaves a chemical deposit around the joints in the body. Worry, fear, anger, jealousy, and other emotional conditions, are mental in their nature, and as such are being recognized as the hidden cause of a large part of all the physical suffering to which the flesh is heir. A normal healthy mind reflects itself in a healthy body, and conversely, an abnormal mental state expresses its corresponding condition in some physical condition. Thoughts are things!

Modern psychology affirms that all the thoughts and emotions we have experienced since we came into conscious existence are still present in Mind, where ceaselessly active, they manifest themselves as subjective tendencies that mold the body in health or sickness; and determine, as well, our reactions to all life and experience.

We do not maintain that this or that specific disease is always the result of thinking about such a condition; but we do assert that a prolonged discordant mental state is certain to eventuate in some form of physical ailment. People have died of great grief; of broken hearts; of outbursts of temper; of deep and continued resentment; of excessive worry, and many other mental states, in which there was no specific thought of sickness at all. The point to remember is, *that all mind activity inevitably tends to create its physical correspondent*, so that an unhealthful and morbid mental state projects itself into the physical body.

Thoughts are things, they have the power to objectify themselves; thought lays hold of Causation and forms real Substance. The word of man is the law of his life, under the One Great Law of all Life. Thoughts of sickness can make a man sick, and thoughts of health and perfection can heal him. Thought is the conscious activity of the one thinking, and works as he directs, through Law; and this Law may be consciously set in motion. This Law will work for him to the fullest extent of his belief in, and understanding of, It. A realization of the Presence of God is the most powerful healing agency known to the mind of man.

# ONE WITH GOD

U ntil we awake to the fact that we are One in nature with God, we shall not find the way of life. Until we realize that our own word has the power of life, we will not see clearly. The Bible points out that man has the same power, in his own life and in his own world, that it claims for God. "The Word was with God and the Word was God," is an oft-repeated but little understood statement. The promise to man is equally positive: "The word is nigh thee, even in thine own mouth that thou shouldst know it and do it." If any word has power, it follows that all words have power. It means that every word which we hear, speak or think, has some power.

# THE POWER WITHIN

T hrough spiritual discernment, we see that we have within us a power which is greater than anything we shall ever contact; a power that can overcome every obstacle in our experience and set us safe, satisfied, and at peace, healed and prosperous in a new light and a new life. "If God be for us who can be against us?"

God's Creative Power of Mind is right here. We have as much of this power to use as we believe in and embody. The storehouse of nature is filled with infinite good, awaiting the touch of our awakened thought to spring forth into manifestation in our lives; but *the awakening must be within our thought!* The word that we speak is the law of our lives, and nothing hinders its operation but ourselves. We may use this creative word for whatever purpose we desire, and this word becomes the law unto the thing for which it was spoken. We are given the power to sit in the midst of our lives and direct their activities. Strife and struggle are unnecessary. We only need to *know*, but we must know *constructively*.

Just so far as we depend upon any condition, past, present or future, we are creating chaos, because we are then dealing with conditions (effects) and not with causes. Could we but comprehend the fact that there is a Power that makes things directly out of Itself—by simply becoming the thing It makes—could we but grasp this greatest truth about life; and realize that we are dealing with a Principle, scientifically correct and eternally present, *we could accomplish whatever it is possible for us to conceive.* Life externalizes at the level of our thought.

## WE SET OUR OWN LIMITATIONS

Do we desire to live in a world peopled with friends who love us, surrounded by things beautiful and pleasing? There is but one way, and this way is as certain as that the sun shines. DAILY WE MUST CONTROL ALL THOUGHT THAT DENIES THE REAL; AFFIRM THE DIVINE PRESENCE WITHIN US; then, as the mist disappears before the sun, so shall adversity melt before the shining radiance of our exalted thought!

The Prodigal Son remained a prodigal as long as he chose to do so. When he chose to, he returned to his "Father's house" and was greeted with outstretched hands. So shall our experience be when we return to the world which is perfect; there will be something that will turn to us. We shall behold a new heaven and a new earth, not in some far off place but here and now. "Act as though I am and I will be." The Spirit of Truth will lead us into all good. This is the highroad to the fulfillment of our lives.

There is, then, no limitation outside our own ignorance, and since we can all conceive of a greater good than we have so far experienced, we all have the ability to transcend previous experiences and rise triumphant above them; but *we shall never triumph over them while we persist in going through the old mental reactions.*

## UNDERSTANDING

Before we attempt to improve our conditions; before we proceed further on the subject of *healing* it is necessary that we be certain in our own minds that *thought is creative*, as upon this basis our entire superstructure rests. Since Spirit creates by contemplation— purely mental action—then everything in the manifest world is *some effect* of Its thought. Our own minds are an expression of the Divine Mind and must be of the same essence.

That we find ourselves in an undesirable condition in the face of all this, is merely proof that we have limited ourselves by our very freedom. Shall we not, then, reverse our thinking and take for our starting point the inherent nature of mental powers?

We have gone far in the right direction, when we have determined that *Creation could have originated only in Intelligence*; and have realized further that our own mental power must be the same in kind with the Creativeness of God. Thus we begin to sense, even though dimly, that as our minds become more like the Divine Mind, we shall expand into a greater livingness—*our world created by our consciousness, and our consciousness taking its color from the perception of our relation to the Infinite!*

We should strive toward a perfect vision, a perfect conception. We should expand our thought until it realizes all good, and then cut right through all that *appears* to be, and use this Almighty Power for definite purposes. We should daily feel a deeper union with Life, a greater sense of that Indwelling God—the God of the seen and of the unseen—within us. When we speak into this Mind, we have sown a seed of thought in the Absolute and we may rest in peace. We need not make haste, for it is done unto us as we believe. "In that day they that call upon me, I will answer."

# CHAPTER TWO

# Prayer

## THE DIFFERENCE BETWEEN PRAYER AND TREATMENT

One of the questions most frequently asked about the Science of Mind is, "Are *prayers* and *treatments* identical?" The answer to this question is both *Yes* and *No*.

If when one prays his prayer is a recognition of Spirit's Omniscience, Omnipotence, and Omnipresence, and a realization of man's unity with Spirit, then his prayer is a spiritual treatment.

If, on the other hand, one is holding to the viewpoint that God is some far-off Being, Whom he would approach with doubt in his thought; wondering if by some good luck he may be able to placate God or persuade Him of the wisdom of one's request—*then*, there is but little similarity between *prayer* and *treatment*. Nothing could bring greater discouragement than to labor under the delusion that God is a Being of moods, who might answer *some* prayers and not others.

It would be difficult to believe in a God who cares more for one person than another. There can be no God who is kindly disposed one day and cruel the next; there can be no God who creates us with tendencies and impulses we can scarcely comprehend, and then eternally punishes us when we make mistakes. God is a Universal Presence, an impersonal Observer, a Divine and impartial Giver, forever pouring Himself into His Creation.

# LAWS GOVERNING PRAYER

Most men who believe in God believe in prayer; but our idea of prayer changes as our idea of God changes; and it is natural for each to feel that his way of praying is the correct way. But we should bear in mind that the prayers which are effective—no matter whose prayers they may be—*are effective because they embody certain universal principles which, when understood, can be consciously used.*

IF GOD EVER ANSWERED PRAYER, HE ALWAYS ANSWERS PRAYER, since He is "the same yesterday, today and forever." If there seems to be any failure, it is in man's ignorance or misunderstanding of the Will and Nature of God.

We are told that "God is Spirit, and they that worship Him must worship Him in spirit and in truth." The immediate availability of the Divine Spirit is "neither in the mountain nor at the temple; neither Lo, here, nor lo there, for behold the Kingdom of God is within."

This is a true perception of spiritual power. The power is no longer I, but "the Father who dwelleth in me." Could we conceive of Spirit as being incarnate in us—while at the same time being ever *more* than that which is incarnated—would we not expand spiritually and intellectually? Would not our prayers be answered before they were uttered? "The Kingdom of God is within you." When we become conscious of our Oneness with Universal Good, beliefs in evil, sin, sickness, limitation, and death tend to disappear. We shall no longer "ask amiss," supplicating as though God were not willing, begging as though He were withholding.

"If ye abide in me and my words abide in you, ye shall ask what ye will and it shall be done unto you." This gives great light on an important law governing the answering of prayer. *Abiding in Him*, means having no consciousness separate from His consciousness—nothing in our thought which denies the power and presence of Spirit. Yes, we can readily see why prayers are answered when we are *abiding in Him*.

Again we read, "Whatsoever ye shall ask in my name, that will I do." This sounds simple at first, but it is another profound statement like unto the first; its significance lies in the phrase: "in my name." *In His name*, means like His Nature. If our thought is as unsullied as the Mind of God, if we are recognizing our Oneness with God, we cannot pray for other than the good of all men. In such prayer we should not dwell upon evil or adversity. The secret of spiritual power lies in a consciousness of one's union with the Whole, and of the availability of Good. God is accessible to all people.

God manifests Himself through all individuals. No two people are alike; each has a unique place in the universe of Mind; each lives in Mind; each contacts It through his own mentality, in an individual way, drawing from It a unique expression of Its Divine Nature. If one makes himself receptive to the idea of love, he becomes lovable. To the degree that he embodies love, he is love; so people who love are loved. Whoever becomes receptive to the idea of peace, poise and calm—whoever embodies these divine realities—finds them flowing through him and he becomes peaceful, poised and calm.

There is a place in us which lies open to the Infinite; but when the Spirit brings Its gift, by pouring Itself through us, It can give to us only what we take. This taking is mental. If we persist in saying that Life will not give us that which is good ("God will not answer *my* prayer"), it cannot, *for Life must reveal Itself to us through our intelligence.* The pent-up energy of life, and the possibility of further human evolution, work through man's imagination and will. *The time is now; the place is where we are, and it is done unto us as we believe.*

## PRAYER IS ESSENTIAL TO HAPPINESS

Prayer is not an act of overcoming God's reluctance, but should be an *active* acceptance of His highest willingness. Through prayer we recognize a spiritual law, that has always existed, and put ourselves in alignment with it. The law of electricity might have been used by Moses had he understood this law. Emerson said: "Is not prayer a study of truth, a sally of the Soul into the unfound Infinite?"

Prayer is constructive, because it enables us to establish closer contact with the Fountain of Wisdom, and we are less likely to be influenced by appearances around us—to judge "according to appearance." Righteous prayer sets the "law of the Spirit of Life" in motion for us.

Prayer is essential, not to the salvation of the soul, for the soul is never lost; but to the conscious well-being of the soul that does not understand itself. There is a vitality in our communion with the Infinite, which is productive of the highest good. As fire warms the body, as food strengthens us, as sunshine raises our spirits, so there is a subtle transfusion of some invisible force in such communion, weaving itself into the very warp and woof of our own mentalities. This conscious commingling of our thought with Spirit is essential to the well-being of every part of us.

Prayer has stimulated countless millions of people to higher thoughts and nobler deeds. That which tends to connect our minds with the Universal Mind lets in a flood of Its consciousness. If we think of God as a Heavenly Dictator—something apart from that which lives and moves and has Its being where we are—then we are certain to believe ourselves disconnected from this Infinite Presence; and the inevitable consequence of such thinking would be a terrible fear that we should *never* be able to make contact with Him! But if we know God as an Indwelling Presence, our prayer is naturally addressed to this Presence in us. We long for, and need, a conscious union with the Infinite. This is as necessary to the nature and intellect of man, as food is to the well-being of his physical body.

## PRAYER IS ITS OWN ANSWER

C ause and effect are but two sides of thought, and Spirit, being ALL, is both Cause and Effect. Prayer, then, is its own answer. The Bible tells us: "Before they call will I answer." Before our prayer is framed in words, God has already answered, *but if our prayer is one of partial belief, then there is only a tendency toward its answer;* if the next day we wholly doubt, then there is no answer at all. In dealing with Mind, we are dealing with a Force we cannot fool. We cannot cheat Principle out of the slightest shadow of our most subtle concept. The hand writes and passes on, but the writing remains; and the only thing that can erase it is writing of a different character. There is no obstruction one cannot dissipate by the power of Truth.

So we learn to go deeply within ourselves, and speak as though there were a Presence there that knows; and we should take the time to unearth this hidden cause, to penetrate this inner chamber of consciousness. It is most worthwhile to commune with Spirit—to sense and feel it. The approach to Spirit is direct . . . through our own consciousness.

This Spirit flows through us. Whatever intelligence we have is this Spirit in us. Prayer is its own answer.

We can be certain that there is an Intelligence in the Universe to which we may come, that will guide and inspire us, a love which overshadows. God is real to the one who believes in the Supreme Spirit, real to the soul that senses its unity with the Whole.

Every day and every hour we are meeting the eternal realities of life, and in such degree as we co-operate with these eternal realities in love, in peace, in wisdom and in joy—believing and receiving—we are automatically blessed. Our prayer is answered before it is uttered.

CHAPTER THREE

# *Faith*

## THE MENTAL APPROACH

The Universe is a Spiritual System. Its laws are those of intelligence. We approach it through the mind, which enables us to know, will and act. Prayer, faith and belief are closely related mental attitudes.

Prayer is a mental approach to Reality. It is not the symbol but *the idea symbolized* that makes prayer effective. Some prayers are more effective than others. Some only help us to endure, while others transcend conditions, and demonstrate an invisible law which has power over the visible. In so far as our prayer is affirmative, it is creative of the desired results.

## ALWAYS A POWER

Faith has been recognized as a power throughout the ages—whether it be faith in God, faith in one's fellowmen, in oneself, or in what one is doing. The idea that faith has only to do with our religious experience is a mistake. Faith is a faculty of the mind that finds its highest expression in the religious attitude, but always the man who has faith in his own ability accomplishes far more than the one who has no confidence in himself. Those who have great faith, have great power.

Why is it that one man's prayers are answered, while another's remain unanswered? It cannot be that God desires more good for one person than another. It must be that all persons, in their approach to Reality, receive results—not because of what they believe in, but because of their belief. Faith is an affirmative mental approach to Reality.

## MISPLACED FAITH

Someone has said that the entire world is suffering from one big fear . . . the fear that God will not answer our prayers. Let us analyze the fears which possess us and see if this is true. The fear of lack is nothing more than the belief that God does not, and will not, supply us with whatever we need. The fear of death is the belief that the promises of eternal life may not be true. The fear of loss of health, loss of friends, loss of property—all arise from the belief that God is not all that we claim: Omniscience, Omnipotence, and Omnipresence.

But what is fear? *Nothing more nor less than the negative use of faith . . .* faith misplaced; a belief in two powers instead of One; a belief that there can be a Power—opposed to God—whose influence and ability *may* bring us evil. In other words, *to correct all the evils of the world, would be but to have the positive faith*, faith rightly placed, a faith that lays hold of the integrity of the Universe, the beneficence of God and the Unity of all life. Nevertheless, we cannot have faith in that which we do not in some measure understand.

## UNDERSTANDING FAITH

We wish a faith based on the knowledge that there is nothing to fear! "Faith is the substance of things hoped for, the evidence of things not seen." The thought of faith molds the undifferentiated substance, and brings into manifestation the thing which was fashioned in the mind. This is how faith brings our desires to pass.

When we use our creative imagination in strong faith, it will create for us, out of the One Substance, whatever we have formed in thought. In this way man becomes a Co-Creator with God. There will never be an end to any of the eternal verities like Truth, Love, Beauty. There will never be an end to God, nor to any of the attributes which are co-eternal and co-existent with God. If we are wise, we shall cultivate a faith in these realities. This is not a difficult *task*, but a thrilling *experience*.

Spiritual Substance is all around us, waiting to be formed. Thus we see what Jesus meant when he said: "And I say unto you, Ask and it shall be given unto you." The Law must work in compliance with our demand. The Divine Urge within us is God's way of letting us know that we should push forward and take that which is awaiting our demand. *If the good were not already ours in the invisible supply, it would be impossible for us to procure it in any manner.* "He openeth his hand and satisfieth the desire of every living creature."

## NO CONFUSION

History has recorded many instances of healing through faith. This is an undisputed fact. Yet we cannot believe in a Divine Power that responds more quickly to one than to another. We are compelled to see that prayer is not an end of itself; it is a means to an end. Like the practice of the Science of Mind, it is *a way*. The principle governing faith is, that when the one praying becomes convinced his prayer will automatically be answered. Jesus announced the law of mind, saying: "It is done unto you as you believe." The Universe exists by Its own self-pronouncement, by Its own affirmation. It only knows "I AM." It knows nothing else. Therefore, wherever prayer, in faith, touches Reality, prays aright—prays according to whatever the Truth is—*then prayer must be answered.*

# AVAILABLE TO ALL

Persons familiar with Biblical history hardly need a lesson about faith, for the eleventh chapter of Hebrews is full of instances proving its sustaining power. Paul enumerates at length the experiences of Enoch, Noah, Abraham, Moses, Gideon, Samuel and the prophets, and many more, "who through faith subdued kingdoms, wrought righteousness, obtained promises, stopped the mouths of lions, quenched the power of fire, escaped the edge of the sword; out of weakness were made strong, waxed mighty in power, turned to flight armies of aliens, women received their dead raised to life again."

Our ancestors believed these records and embodied this living faith in their consciousness, thereby leaving us a great legacy of faith. Whatever they did, they were able to do because they grasped an instinctive faith and marched boldly on with it.

Since faith is a quality unconfined to age or station, it may be ours today as much as it has been any man's at any time. We are not going through a harder time today, a longer or darker night, than has ever been experienced before. It only seems darker because we have lost faith—the beacon light.

If one will have faith in himself, faith in his fellowmen, in the Universe, and in God, that faith will light the place in which he finds himself, and by the light of this faith, he will be able to see that ALL IS GOOD. And the light shed by this faith will light the way for others. We become conscious of darkness only when we are without faith—for faith is ever the light of our day and the light on our way, making that way clearly visible to us, even when to all others it may be beset with obstacles and the ongoing rough.

## VITALIZING FAITH

In order to *have* faith, we must have a conviction that all is well. In order to *keep* faith, we must allow nothing to enter our thought which will weaken this conviction. Faith is built up from belief, acceptance and trust. Whenever anything enters our thought which destroys, in any degree, one of these attitudes, to that extent faith is weakened.

Our mind must be steady in its conviction that our life is some part of God, and that the Spirit is incarnated in us. Affirmations and denials are for the purpose of vitalizing faith—for the purpose of converting thought to *a belief* in things spiritual. The foundation for correct mental treatment is perfect God, perfect man, and perfect being. Thought must be organized to fit this premise, and conclusions must be built on this premise. We must keep our faith vital, if we hope to successfully treat for ourselves or others.

All sciences are built upon *faith principles*. All principles are invisible, and all laws accepted on faith. No man has seen God at any time, nor has he seen goodness, truth or beauty, but who can doubt their existence?

Not only must we have complete faith in Spirit, and Its ability to know and to do, but we must have complete confidence in our approach to It. We must not be lukewarm in our conviction. *We must know that we know.* We are to demonstrate that spiritual thought force has power over all apparent material resistance, and this cannot be done unless we have abounding confidence in the Principle which we approach.

Pure faith is a spiritual conviction; it is the acquiescence of the mind, the embodiment of an idea, the acceptance of a concept. If we believe that the Spirit, incarnated in us, can demonstrate, shall we be disturbed at what *appears* to contradict this? We shall often need to *know* that the Truth which we announce is superior to the condition we are to change. In other words, *if we are speaking from the standpoint of the Spirit, then there can be no opposition to It!* It is only when we let go of all human will, and recognize the pure essence of the Spiritual Principle incarnated in us, that thought rises above a belief in duality. We should constantly vitalize our faith by the knowledge that the Eternal is incarnated in us; that God Himself goes forth anew into creation through each one of us; and that in such degree as we speak the Truth, the Almighty has spoken!

# THE TECHNIQUE OF
# ACQUIRING FAITH

One cannot be a good student of the Science of Mind who is filled with fear and confusion. He must keep himself in a state of equilibrium, in a state of poise, peace and confidence . . . in a state of spiritual understanding. By *spiritual understanding*, is not meant anything strange or unnatural, but merely that the belief in goodness must be greater than any apparent manifestation of its opposite. It is this science of faith we are seeking to uncover—a definite technique that will conduct our minds through a process of thought, if necessary, to that place which the sublime minds of all ages have reached by direct intuition.

There is no one who believes more in faith, more in prayer, or more in the necessity of the Divine Will being done, than he who practices daily the Science of Mind. He has relieved his mind of the morbid sense that the Will of God *can* be the will of suffering; for if there were a suffering God, and if we are eternal beings, then we should suffer through all eternity. But a suffering God is an impossibility. We suffer because we are not in both conscious and subjective communication with the affirmative side of the Universe. All human misery is a result of ignorance; and nothing but knowledge can free us from this ignorance and its effect.

As students of the Science of Mind, we find in the remarkable character of Jesus, a great impetus toward faith and conviction. The Centurion came to Jesus and asked Him to heal his servant, and Jesus said: "Go thy way; and as thou hast believed, so be it done unto thee." The Centurion had what we call a mental equivalent of Divine Authority. In the realm in which he lived, he was accustomed to speak his word with authority. He accepted the word of Jesus as having authority on the invisible plane. Jesus said, "I have not found so great faith, no, not in all Israel."

It is wonderful to contemplate the mental attitude of people who are not afraid to believe their prayers will be answered, and are not afraid to say, "I know." We shall all arrive at this same assurance, this perfect faith, in such degree as we cease contemplating the Universe as opposed to Itself; as we cease having the will to do or to be that which is contrary to the Universal Good.

There is nothing in the universal order that denies the individual's good, or self-expression, so long as such self-expression does not contradict the general good, does not contradict Goodness Itself. There is nothing in the Universe that denies us the right to be happy, if our happiness does not deny or interfere with the general good. The Universe remains unlimited, though the whole world has suffered a sense of limitation.

We should be careful not to divide our mental house against itself. Having announced the law of liberty, we must not deny it. When we shall all know the Truth, then ways and means and methods will be found for the freedom of all. The mold of acceptance is the measure of our experience. The Infinite fills all molds and forever flows into new and greater ones. Within us is the unborn possibility of limitless experience. Ours is the privilege of giving birth to it!

# CONVICTION

Mental Science does not deny the divinity of Jesus; but it does affirm the divinity of all people. It does not deny that Jesus was the son of God; but it affirms that all men are the sons of God. It does not deny that the kingdom of God was revealed through Jesus; but it says that the kingdom of God is also revealed through you and me.

Jesus said: "If ye have faith as a grain of mustard seed, ye shall say unto this mountain, remove hence to yonder place, and it shall remove; and nothing shall be impossible unto you." Faith is centered in, and co-operates with, Divine Mind.

Because we fail to realize that Principle is not bound by precedent, we limit our faith to that which has already been accomplished, and few "miracles" result. When, through intuition, faith finds its proper place under Divine Law, there are no limitations, and what are called *miraculous* results follow.

While Jesus remained with the disciples, their faith for the most part was of the same essence as his, but as the years passed and his followers became more and more immersed in objective organization, they ceased to preach the necessity of a living faith. In fact, a few hundred years later, the Christians were teaching that the early "miracles" merely proved the divinity of Jesus!

If we are to have an active faith—the faith *of* God instead of merely a faith *in* God—our thought must be centered in Universal Mind. We are convinced that under Divine Law all things are possible, if we only *believe*, and work in conformity with the principles of that Law. Such a faith does not spring full-orbed into being, but grows by knowledge and experience. No matter what the outside appearance, we must cling steadfastly to the knowledge that God is good, and God is all, underneath, above and round about. Thus we shall be able to say, with conviction: "I know in whom I have believed. . . ."

CHAPTER FOUR

# Mental and
# Spiritual Treatment

## TREATMENT: WHAT IT IS

Effective mental treatment is propelled by a consciousness of love and a realization that the Creative Spirit is always at work. The practitioner does not feel that he must compel the Force to work. It is the nature of the Creative Power to take form, and it is the nature of man to use It.

A treatment should be given in a calm, expectant manner and with a deep inner conviction of its reality, without any fear or any sense that the human mind must make it effective. The work is effective because the Law is always in operation.

# THE *PURPOSE* OF TREATMENT

Mental or spiritual treatment should bring into actual manifestation the health and happiness which are mankind's normal and divine heritage. Such healing includes the emancipation of the mind from every form of bondage through a new concept of God, which causes the heart to beat with joy and gladness. This healing power is a consciousness of the Unity of all Life and the spiritual nature of all being. Man's life is rooted in the Universal and the Eternal, which life is none other than the Life of God. The healing process, in so far as it may be termed a process, is in becoming conscious of this eternal truth.

Treatment should incorporate a *conscious recognition* that health has always been ours, abundance has always been ours, happiness and peace have always been ours; they are ours now, for they are the very essence and Truth of our being. All there is of evil, of whatever name or kind, is an inversion of eternal good.

# THE *WAY* OF TREATMENT

In treatment, we turn entirely away from the condition, because as long as we look at it, we cannot overcome it. By thinking upon a condition, we tend to animate it with the life of our thought, and thereby it is perpetuated and magnified. Treatment is the science of inducing, within Mind, concepts, acceptances and realizations of peace, poise, power, plenty—health, happiness and success—or whatever the particular need may be.

Treatment is not *willing* things to happen; it is to provide within ourselves an avenue through which they may happen. Treatment opens up the avenues of thought, expands the consciousness, and lets Reality through; it clarifies the mentality, removes the obstruction of thought and lets in the Light; it removes doubt and fear, in the realization of the Presence of Spirit, and is necessary while we are confronted by obstructions or obstacles. We already live in a Perfect Universe, but It needs to be seen mentally before It can become a part of our experience. Every problem is primarily mental, and the answer to all problems will be found in Spiritual Realization.

It is hardly necessary to state here that without an understanding of the limitless medium of Subjectivity there can be no full comprehension of how Law operates, when a treatment is given. Unless we understand the three-fold nature of both man and the Universe: as active consciousness, which we call Spirit; receptive or creative Law, which we call the medium or Universal Subjectivity; and manifestation, which we call form or Creation . . . unless we realize further, that as we deal with our own individuality, we are dealing with the Universal, which has projected out of Itself that which is like Itself on a miniature scale . . . unless we have this understanding, we shall be working much of the time on a basis of blind faith.

As an illustration of the importance of this understanding, take the following: Suppose a man in New York wired a practitioner in

Los Angeles, explaining to him that he had been unable to sleep for
weeks and that he wished treatment for insomnia. How would the
practitioner go about this? The practitioner in Los Angeles knows
that the man in New York fails to sleep because there is lack of peace
in his consciousness; there is a mental disturbance, and the mind
keeps working all night. The practitioner begins to think *peace* about
this man. He does *not* say: "Now, John [supposing the man's name is
John], you are going to be peaceful"; rather, he says *to himself*, "John
*is* peaceful." The practitioner does not send out thoughts nor sugges-
tions; he realizes, in his own mind, the truth about this man. *The
practitioner treats the practitioner, for the patient, always!* The practitioner begins to pour the uplifting truth into his own mind: "John
sleeps in peace, wakes in joy, and lives in good. There is no fear, no
worry, no doubt, no confusion. He has not acquired the habit of
wakefulness, because his consciousness is filled with peace."

Universal Mind, being Omnipresent, is wherever the man is who
asked for help. If he is receptive to the harmony of the belief which
the practitioner has poured into Subjective Mind, it will externalize
for him at the level of the embodiment of the thought of the practitioner. Thus the man "John" in New York is helped through the work
of the practitioner in Los Angeles.

A practitioner works through the Law of Mind, definitely, for
someone else. He declares the truth about the person whom he is
treating, stating that this person is a Divine Being, complete, happy,
satisfied, conscious of his own spiritual being; that this thing which is
causing him to suffer now is not a law, has no right to be, is no longer

effective through him, cannot suggest anything to him; that he is free from it; that this word—which the practitioner is speaking—removes any obstruction in mind, or obstruction in manifestation, and allows the flow of life through this individual. He makes such statements to himself, about this individual, as tend to clear up, in his own thought, his belief about the person whom he is treating, until finally he comes to a place in his treatment where he says that the person is *now* all right; he is free from that condition. It can never return. That this is the Truth about him; that this *now* is the Truth. This is a formed treatment, stated definitely—a scientific treatment.

To the average person, when a result is obtained by this method of work, it looks as though a miracle has happened, but such is not the case. It is only a miracle as everything else in life is a miracle. A definite, conscious idea has been set in motion in the Subjective World, which accepts ideas at their own valuation and tends to act upon them.

# TREATMENT NOT EXPLAINED IN THE BIBLE

From beginning to end, in one way or another, the Bible teaches the law of cause and effect, based upon the premise that the Universe is a spiritual system, that man is included in this spiritual system, that the Infinite creates by the power of Its word or the contemplation of Its consciousness, and, as a complement to this, that man reproduces the Universal on an individual scale.

*The Bible does not tell us how to give a treatment.* It is only within the last hundred years that the science which we are studying has been given to the world. It is not an old system of thought. The old systems of thought did contain the Truth, but one would never learn *how* to give an effective mental treatment by studying them. We would no more learn how to give a treatment by studying the Bible, than we would learn how to psycho-analyze a person. The principle of spiritual treatment is implied in the Bible as well as in other sacred writings of antiquity, but one could not learn how to give a treatment from reading any of these Sacred Books. From all of these sources we gain a tremendous spiritual inspiration, *but they do not teach how to give a treatment.*

## WHAT IS A PRACTITIONER?

The one who attempts to heal himself or another through a recognition of the creative power of Mind and the ever availability of Good, is a mental or spiritual practitioner. Such a one refuses to allow negative thoughts to control his consciousness. He endeavors to greet the divinity in every man he meets.

The one seeking to demonstrate the power of spiritual realization in everyday affairs should believe in Divine guidance. He should affirm that his mind is continually impressed with the images of right action, and that everything in his life is controlled by love, harmony and peace; that everything he does prospers, and that the

Eternal Energy back of all things animates everything which he undertakes. Every objective evidence contrary to good should be resolutely denied, and in its place should come a sense of right action. He should feel a unity of Spirit in all people, and running through all events. He should declare that the Spirit within him is God, quickening into right action everything he touches, bringing the best out of all his experiences, and forever guiding and sustaining. The greatest good which his mind is able to conceive should be affirmed as a part of his everyday experience. No matter what the occupation of such a man, he is a mental and spiritual practitioner, and from such daily meditation he should venture forth into a life of action, with the will to do, the determination to be, and a joy in becoming!

The *professional* mental and spiritual practitioner is one who has dedicated his life—his time, his energies, his intelligence—to helping others, through mental and spiritual means and methods.

## THE FIRST REQUISITE

The first requisite for the mental and spiritual practitioner is a full sense of the sacredness of his trust; the sacredness of the confidence of his patient, which impels him to pour out his very soul. *This confidence, a practitioner should keep sacred, inviolate.* He should no more betray this trust than would a priest who officiates at the confessional, a lawyer who handles the business and finances

of his client, or a physician who cares for the physical well being of
his patients.

Practitioners do meet occasionally and discuss cases, as doctors
might in a clinic, but they should never mention the names nor the
personal affairs of those under treatment.


# A PRACTITIONER'S BUSINESS

It is the practitioner's business to uncover God in every man. God
is not sick. God is not poor. God is not unhappy. God is never
afraid. God is never confused. God is never out of His place. The
premise upon which all mental work is based is perfect God, perfect
man, perfect being.

First, perfect God, then perfect man. There is a spiritual man
who is never sick, who is never poor, unhappy; never confused nor
afraid . . . who is never caught by negative thought. Browning called
this "the spark which a man may desecrate but never quite lose."

These are the tools of thought with which a practitioner works.
Where does he do his work? IN HIS OWN MIND. Never anywhere
else. Always in his own thought. A practitioner never tries to get
away from the mind within.

We are practicing scientifically when the mind refuses to see the
apparent condition and turns to the Absolute. A scientific treatment
cannot be conditioned upon anything that now exists, upon any
experience less than perfection. In treatment, we turn entirely away

from the relative—entirely away from that which appears to be. We might begin a treatment with the statement: "With God all things are possible, God can find a way." We might say: "They that dwell in the Secret Place of the Most High," etc. It does not matter so much what one says, it is what one believes when he says it that counts. He must *believe*, if he is going to be a successful practitioner, that his word is the law of that whereunto it is spoken.

We treat man, not as a patient, not as a physical body, not as a diseased condition; neither do we treat the disease as belonging to him. We must not think of the disease as being connected with him or as any part of him. The practitioner realizes that man is born of Spirit and not of matter. He realizes this until he sees his patient a living embodiment of Perfection.

A practitioner, then, is one who, recognizing the power of Mind, definitely, specifically, concretely and consciously speaks from his objective mind into Subjectivity and gives direction to a Law, which is the Actor.

What the practitioner really does is to take his patient, the disease and everything that appears to be wrong, into his own mentality, and here he attempts to dissolve all false appearances and all erroneous conclusions. At the center of the practitioner's own being, the healing work must be accomplished.

The more completely the practitioner is convinced of the power of his own word, the more power his word will have. THERE MUST BE A RECOGNITION THAT THE POWER OF THE WORD, OPERATING AS THE TRUTH AND REALITY OF BEING, CAN

DO ALL THINGS. Therefore, the person whose consciousness is the clearest, who has the most complete faith, will be the best healer.

## DIFFERENT METHODS OF TREATMENT

Although several methods of treatment are used, there are but two distinct methods; one is called the *argumentative* and the other *realization*.

The argumentative method is just what the word implies, though the argument is never with another person—it is a process of mental reasoning in which the practitioner argues to himself about his patient. He is presenting a logical argument to Universal Mind, or Principle, and if it carries with it complete evidence in favor of his patient, the patient should be healed.

The realization method is one whereby the practitioner realizes within himself—without the necessity of step by step building up a conclusion—the perfect state of his patient. It is purely a spiritual and meditative process of contemplating the perfect man, and if the practitioner arrives at a perfect embodiment of the idea, without confusion or doubt, it will at once produce a healing. *Treatment is for the purpose of inducing an inner realization of perfection in the mentality of the practitioner, which inner realization, acting through Mind, operates through the patient.*

Another illustration: Let us suppose that Mary is sick and John is the practitioner. She comes to him, saying: "I am sick." He understands the power of Mind; she does not understand it. He does not try to hold a thought over her or for her, nor suggest one to her. He speaks her name and makes his declarations about this name. He contradicts what appears to be wrong and declares the Truth about her. What happens? *His word, operative through Universal Mind, sets a law in motion, on the subjective side of life, which objectifies through her body as healing.*

Mary thinks a miracle has been performed. No miracle has been enacted. John used a law, which all men may use if they will. If Mary had been perfectly well, and her need had been for a position, the treatment would be of like nature; John would have declared into Mind what should be done for Mary. There is only One Law; Mary could set It in operation for herself if she understood Its nature; sooner or later she must come to understand and make conscious use of this Law.

*Between* "John" and "Mary" there is One Universal Medium, which is also *in* John and *in* Mary. It is not only between them but in them and around them. As John, right where he is, knows the Truth, since there is only One, he is at the same time knowing the Truth *right where Mary is*, because his work is operative through a field which is not divided, but a complete Unit or Whole. As he knows within himself, he is knowing within the same Mind which operates through the person whom he mentions in his treatment, no matter where that person may be. There is no *absent* treatment, as opposed to a *present* treatment. When you know in one place, you know everywhere. When you give a treatment, you never send out a thought, or hold a thought, or make a suggestion. *A treatment is a conscious movement of thought, and the work begins and ends in the thought of the one giving the treatment. The practitioner must do the work within himself.* He must know the Truth within himself, and as he does this the Law unfolds; a thing which is known by any part of Universal Mind is known by every part of It, for It is an undivided Whole.

If one were treating "Henry Black," who is in another city, he would say: "I am treating Henry Black of such-and-such a place." Then he would forget all about Henry Black as a personality and give the treatment. It is not necessary to specify the trouble. Occasionally, there might be reason to mention a thing, in denying its existence, but this is not the best method. Of course, there are certain thoughts back of certain things, and a knowledge of the disease might better enable some practitioners to know what thought to deny.

Another illustration of the difference between the *argumentative* method of treatment and the *realization* method, will be found in the following:

*Mary Jones* comes to *John Smith* and says, "I have tuberculosis." In answer to this, he states: "The word I now speak is for Mary Jones. She is a perfect and complete manifestation of Pure Spirit, and Pure Spirit cannot be diseased, consequently, she is not diseased." This is an argument in the mind of "John Smith" trying to bring out the evidence in favor of "Mary Jones's" perfection; it is an argument which produces certain conclusions in his mind, and as a result it sets a certain law in motion for Mary Jones. As John does this, day after day, he gradually becomes convinced of her spiritual perfection. This is the *argumentative* method of treating. *All argumentative statements merely conduct the mind of the practitioner to a place where he believes what he is saying!*

In using the method of *realization*, "John Smith" would say: "The word that I now speak is for Mary Jones." Then he would begin to realize the Perfect Presence, the ONLY Perfect Presence. "God is all there is; there is nothing else. God is in Mary Jones, she is now a perfect being, she is now a spiritual being."

It makes no difference, however, which method one uses as each produces the same results. One method is a logical argument in the mind of the practitioner, by which he convinces himself of the Truth of Being; the other is the instant cutting through of all appearances to the Reality back of all things. Undoubtedly, when we can pursue only the way of *pure realization*, we will have attained the ideal method.

But since we do not at all times realize man's perfection, we go through this process called "treating" to find it out. Do not be afraid of this scientific approach; do not be afraid to set down on one side all of the negative appearances, admitting them as a condition; and on the other side bringing all the arguments, one at a time, which offset these apparent conditions, and finally realization will come.

This *argumentative* method of treatment is a series of affirmations and denials, for the purpose of building up in the mind of the practitioner a state of realization and acceptance. The power is in the realization, but there is also power in the argument. The one giving the treatment believes that there is a Power and a Presence that responds to his thought. No matter what all the world believes, no matter what anyone says, *he must believe that this Power does respond to his word.* As Jesus said, "Heaven and earth shall pass away, but my words shall not pass away." This is conviction, and if a practitioner does not have such conviction he must acquire it. After much experience, he will learn how best to build up a faith in the Power of Spirit. We are to approach this Presence simply, directly and easily, for It is *within us.* We can never get outside ourselves; we shall always be interior in our comprehension, we are here and It also is here.

In giving spiritual treatments we find that the more completely the mind turns away from lack, the more completely the thought stops trying to figure out how the demonstration can be made, the more completely it refrains from will power, and, strange as it may seem, the less it tries to concentrate, THE MORE POWER IT HAS. Treatment has nothing to do with any effort which attempts to concentrate the Energy of God. The Energy of God is already concentrated *everywhere.* The gardener does not *will* potatoes and cabbages into being, but he has a willingness to comply with the law of nature, and provides the conditions which make it possible for this law to produce them.

# WHEN AND WHAT
# IS A DEMONSTRATION?

In the language of metaphysics, a "demonstration" is made when the thing is accomplished which the one treating desires to achieve . . . whether it be health, happiness or abundance. A demonstration is a manifestation. It is prayer answered. When the word of a practitioner takes form, this is a demonstration. When desire is given a subjective mold and then becomes objectified in the life of the one for whom the practitioner is working, this is demonstration. The practitioner, of course, gives thanks as he makes his demand on the Infinite, knowing that supply and demand are one, and that his request is instantly manifest on the invisible plane. "Before they call, will I answer," is the divine promise.

*We cannot demonstrate beyond our ability to mentally embody an idea.* The argument is between our experience, what the world believes and what we are convinced is the Truth.

It should be understood that we can demonstrate in spite of ourselves—in spite of all weakness, in spite of all fear, in spite of all that is in us—because such is the power of Truth. We wait only for our own awakened thought. The Law is neither good nor bad. Law is and responds.

*The possibility of demonstrating does not depend upon environment, condition, location, personality or opportunity.* It depends solely upon our belief and our acceptance, and our willingness to comply with the Law through which all good comes. The Universe will never deny us anything, unless we conceive that it is possible for us to think of something that is impossible for the Universe to produce! Everyone who asks receives, according to his belief.

## LET US NOT FOOL OURSELVES

B ut we should not fool ourselves about any demonstration. We know there is a state of consciousness which can heal instantly, but if we do not arrive at this in a moment, we should never admit defeat. Let us not despise our sums in addition because we cannot at the outset extract the cube root.

The kind of demonstration we believe in is the kind that can be checked by a physician, if one so desires. If we are treating for the removal of a cancer, we have not made a demonstration until the cancer is gone and the wholeness of the body is evident to anyone. This is not a process of saying "Peace" when there is no peace.

A practitioner working for one whose blood pressure is high might say, "Go every week or so and have your blood pressure tested." If one's blood pressure is high, a demonstration will not have been made until it is reduced to normal. To claim that he is perfectly normal, while the blood pressure remains high, would be to affront the intelligence of any sane individual.

While it is possible that we might have to work on a case for some time, *there should be some sign of improvement from the first treatment.* If the practitioner admits to himself that it is going to take a long time, he is losing sight of the fact that he is dealing with the instantaneous *now* and the ever-present *here.*

Our theory rests entirely upon the supposition that it is impossible to have a true subjective concept, without there being a positive, absolute and equal objective fact. The two will exactly balance. For every action there is always an opposite and equal reaction. If this is true and the equal and opposite reaction is automatic—like a reflection which nothing can stop—then the practitioner does not try to create the reflection; he tries to embody the image. There cannot be an embodiment of the image without the appreciation of what the image means. A man who is always distraught cannot give a good treatment for peace. *So there must not only be the image in the man's mind who is giving the treatment, but there must be an appreciation of what the image means, before the image can reflect itself;* otherwise, it is a word and not an embodiment. There is a great difference between the two. The word which carries power is the one which has conviction back of it. Let us not blithely repeat words, and say the treatment has gone forth and the healing work accomplished, unless we have the evidence that our word has accomplished "that, whereunto it was sent." Let us not deceive ourselves about our treatments.

This matter of self-deception about the truth of a demonstration is the most prolific field for delusion in our system of thought. There is nothing in all our teaching which calls for lying to ourselves or others. The more natural we can be, the more spontaneous we can be, and the more we can discharge the obligation of giving the treatment without taking on the responsibility of healing the condition—of putting the power into the treatment—the more power we shall have.

There is nothing in the world more specific than a scientific treatment, but there is nothing that should be so released from outline as a scientific treatment. However, there is no secret in this business of demonstrating. The only secret is the persistent ability to use the Law, and the determination to continue to use It until we prove It.

# Spiritual Mind Healing

*Ideation: A Recognition of the Power,
and the Thought and Purpose back of Mind Healing*

The possibility of spiritual mind healing, changing environment, controlling conditions, etc., through the power of right thinking, rests entirely upon the theory that we are surrounded by a Universal Mind, which reacts to our thought—and always according to Law.

Spiritual Man is Perfect, but his individual use of Life and Law enables him to cover a perfect idea with an apparently imperfect cloak.

Sickness is not a spiritual Reality; it is an experience—an effect and not a cause. The body, devoid of mentality, could neither know nor experience sensation—it is entirely an effect. The body of man is made from the same undifferentiated Spiritual Substance from which all Creation is formed.

Man comes into objectivity with the tendency of the race already subjectified within him, through race-suggestion. The race experiences sickness and limitation, and this suggestion is more or less operative through all people. It works through the subjective race thought and operates through the individual.

Man need not consciously think negation in order to produce physical disturbance, but the physical correspondent is a logical outcome of what he thinks. Thus we see not only how important it is to entertain right thoughts, but also the necessity for having a constructive basis for our thinking.

We find that prayer is essential to happiness, for righteous prayer sets the law of the Spirit of life in motion for our good. Prayer is essential to the conscious well-being of the soul. Prayer has stimulated countless millions to higher thoughts and better lives. Prayer is its own answer. Before our prayer is framed in words the possibility of its answer already exists.

We find that faith in God is a spiritual quality of the mind; and an understanding faith is based on Immutable Principle. Its action is higher than that of the intellect, because it is born of intuition.

One should have faith in himself, faith in his fellowman, in the Universe, and in God. Our mind must be steady in its conviction that our life is some part of God, and that the Spirit is incarnated in us. "Faith is the substance of things hoped for; the evidence of things not seen."

A spiritual practitioner is one who recognizes man as a Spiritual Reality. *Since there is but One Mind, the practitioner makes this recognition within his own mind.* Through the medium of the One Mind, his statements rise to objective conditions in his patient, according

to his belief and the patient's receptivity. Healing is accomplished through the act of setting Subjective Law in motion. The more spiritual or Godlike the mentality of the practitioner, the more powerful the treatment.

A mental treatment begins and ends within the thought of the practitioner, because he is in the same Mind in which his patient lives. Treatment is the act of inducing right concepts on the subjective side of life.

Absent and present treatments are the same, *for there is no absence in the One Presence.* So far as the practitioner is concerned, there is no difference between an absent and a present treatment. He needs only to know whom he wishes to help, realizing that in the field of Mind and Spirit there is no apartness, and then he speaks the word for the other person, in full confidence that the Law will operate upon it. He is not concerned where the person *is* whom he desires to help, or what he may be doing at that particular time. He is concerned only with his own thought relative to this person, endeavoring to bring out in his own mind the realization that this person is a spiritual entity, governed by a perfect Law, directed by positive Intelligence, and animated by Divine Life, Love, and Law.

There is no personal responsibility in healing. We should not feel that *we put the power into the word.* The practitioner directs the Power and lets It work. One does not *hold thought* in mental healing; he looses thought. A practitioner does not try to suggest, hypnotize or mentally influence; he simply seeks to *know* that man *is now* a spiritual being, and he holds to that belief no matter what the appearance may be. Right mental treatment does not tire the one giving the treatment.

Personal magnetism has nothing to do with mental healing. The whole basis of the possibility of mental healing rests upon the premise that we all live in One Creative Mind which reacts to our belief. It is as though there were a Universal Ear, listening to and hearing everything that we say, feel or think, and reacting to it.

Healing is not a process but a revelation; for the revealing of the perfect man always heals. The process, if there is one, is the time and thought that it takes to arrive at the correct understanding of man's perfect state in Spirit.

Anyone can heal who believes that he can, and who will take the time to set that belief in motion through the Law. To daily see the perfect man, and to daily declare for his objective appearance, is correct mental practice and will heal.

A treatment recognizes that all is Mind, and that everything is mental. It dissolves all disease into thought; neutralizes the false thought and recognizes the true. Nothing can stop it from operating except a lack of faith in the reality of Truth and man's ability to use it.

In giving mental treatment, the practitioner first realizes his own being as spiritual; he then recognizes the spiritual state of his patient's being; then he attacks the false claim and brings the evidence of Truth to bear against it, thinking in such a manner as to completely destroy the false claim and realize the Truth. In such degree as this acknowledgment is complete, petition is transmuted into acceptance, and the mind actually feels that the object of its desire is already an accomplished fact.

The greatest good that can come to anyone is the forming within him of an absolute certainty of himself, and of his relationship to the Universe, forever removing the sense of heaven as being outside himself.

Such an understanding teaches us that there can never come a time when we shall stop progressing; that age is an illusion, that limitation is a mistake, that unhappiness is ignorance. This understanding will rob man of his loneliness and give him a sense of security which knows no fear, a peace without which no life can be happy, a poise which is founded on this peace, and a power which is the result of the union of peace with poise.

# Meditations for Self-Help and Healing

I n these short meditations I have tried to set forth some ideas which my experiences in mental healing have given me. I have found that a few brief statements, mentally affirmed, followed by a silent meditation, have been most effective in the healing work.

Most of these meditations have been written in the first person in order that those using them may be able to do so just as they are written.

It is not claimed that there is any occult power in the words, but that words similar to these are effective in inducing a greater realization of life.

First, decide which meditation you wish to use; then become quiet and composed. Then carefully read the meditation several times, phrase by phrase, endeavoring to realize the meaning of the words and trying to enter into the atmosphere of the thought. After

having done this, meditate upon the words, following that meditation until you feel a sense of realization.

## COME, AND LET ME HEAL YOU

Come and I will heal you.

The inner power of Life within me is God,

And God has all power.

I will heal and help all who come to me.

I know that the realization of Life and Love within me heals
all who come into Its presence.

I silently bless all who enter my atmosphere.

It is not I, but the Father Who dwelleth in me, He doeth the
works.

*I heal all who come near me.*

## HE IS MIGHTY WITHIN ME TO HEAL

God within me is mighty to heal.

He healeth me of all my diseases and removes all fear
from me.

My God within is now healing me of all sickness and pain
and is bringing comfort to my soul.

God is my life; I cannot be sick.

I hear the voice of Truth telling me to arise and walk, for I
am healed.

*I am healed.*

### I Do Not Inherit Disease

There is no inherited tendency to disease nor ill health.

I am born of Pure Spirit.

False ideas cannot be transmitted from one to another, and I
am free from race-suggestion.

My Life is from Above, and I remember that I was always
Perfect and Complete.

An Inner Light shines forth and frees me from the bonds of
false belief.

*I came from the Spirit.*

### No Congestion

There is no congestion nor stoppage of action.

Life, flowing through me, is Perfect and Clear;

It cannot be stopped, retarded nor hindered.

I feel the One Life flowing through me now.

It eliminates all impure secretions and cleanses my thought
from any suggestion of false deposits in the flesh.

I am Clean, Pure and Perfect, and my Word eliminates all else.

*There is no congestion.*

### No False Growth

"Every plant which my Heavenly Father hath not planted,
shall be rooted up."

There is no false growth and nothing for one to feed on. I am

free from all thought of, or belief in, anything false or
fearsome.

I cast out all fear and with it all manifestation of fear.

A false idea is neither person, place nor thing, and has no
one to believe in nor experience it.

I am now One with The Perfect Life of Complete
Wholeness.

*My Word casts out all fear.*

## NO WEARINESS

There is no weariness.

Mind and Spirit do not become tired nor weary, and I am
Mind and Spirit.

The flesh cannot become weary, since it has no mind of
its own.

I am free from all illusions of weariness.

My whole being responds to the thought of Life.

I am alive with the Great Vitality of the Spirit.

*I am alive with Spirit.*

## PERFECT HEARING

My hearing is perfect.

It is God in me hearing His own voice.

I hear That Voice, and no belief in inaction can hinder that
hearing.

There are no impaired organs.

Every idea of the body is now complete and perfect and
functions according to the Divine Law.

I open my ears to hear.

I am receptive to Truth and can understand it.

*Open my ears that I may hear.*

## PERFECT VISION

There is One Vision and One perfect seeing.

My eyes are open and I behold Perfect Life.

No suggestion of imperfect vision can enter my
thought.

I perceive that all people can see, and that the One, looking
through all, sees and is not limited in vision.

I am one with a complete understanding of Truth.

I do open my eyes and I do see.

This Word operates even through me and manifests through
my eyes NOW.

*Open my eyes that I may see.*

## THE ALL-SEEING EYE

The Eye of the Spirit cannot be dimmed, neither can It be
limited in Its ability to see.

My eyes are the Vision of my Indwelling Lord; they are the
Windows of my Inner Spirit and are always open to
the Vision of Truth.

I see with the Vision of the Spirit, and this sight cannot be
weakened nor lost; it is forever effective.
My word which I now speak is the Law of Perfect Sight, my
eyes are opened and I see.

*Spirit sees through me.*


## THE HEALING OF THE FLESH

My flesh is the Manifestation of the Spirit in my body.
It is kept perfect through the Law of God.
"In my flesh shall I see God."
The mantle of flesh is perfect and complete here and now.
It is one with the Body of God, and cannot be sick, nor
suffer.

*My flesh is Perfect.*


## THERE IS NO PAIN

There is no pain nor inflammation.
All fear is swept away in the realization of Truth.
I am free from every belief in pain.
The Spirit cannot pain, and I am Pure Spirit.

*I am free from all pain.*


## HAPPINESS AND COMPLETION

I am happy and complete, today and forever.
Within me is that which is Perfect and Complete.

It is the Spirit of all Life, Truth and Action.

I am happy in the certain knowledge of this Inner Light.

I cannot be sad nor sorry, but must radiate Joy and Life, for
Life is within me now.

*I am happy and complete.*

## HERE AND NOW

Perfection is already accomplished.

I am that Perfect Life here and now.

Today I express the Limitless Life of the All Good.

Today I manifest my Completion in every part of me.

Today I am saved.

*Here and now I am healed.*

## MAJESTIC CALM

The Inner Mind is still.

The Soul reflects the Most High.

The Spirit of man is God.

In the great calm of the All Good,

I rest in peace and security.

My life is now reflecting the Perfect Whole.

I am Peace; I am calm.

I am security and complete satisfaction.

I am One with God.

*I am filled with peace.*

## No Loss

There is no loss.

Nothing can be lost, misplaced nor forgotten.

There was never any loss nor confusion.

Creation is Perfect and Complete, within the One are all
    things, and all are known to the One.

I am now in complete harmony with the Whole and I cannot
    lose nor misplace anything.

I am constantly finding more and more Good.

*I know that there is no loss.*


## Oh, for a Tongue to Express

Oh, for a tongue to express the Wonders which the Thought
    reveals!

Oh, for some Word to comprehend the boundless idea!

Would that some Voice were sweet enough to sound the
    harmony of Life.

But Within, in that vast realm of thought where the Soul
    meets God, the Spirit knows.

I will listen for that Voice and It will tell me of Life, of Love
    and Unity.

*Speak to me, Spirit.*


## O Soul of Mine, Look Out and See

O Soul of mine, look out and see; look up and know Thy
    freedom.

Be not cast down nor dismayed; be uplifted within me and
exult, for Thy Salvation has come.
Behold the wonders of the Great Whole and the marvels of
the Universe.
Look out and see Thy good. It is not afar off, but is at hand.
Prepare Thyself to accept and believe; to know and live.
Let Life enter and live through Thee, Soul of mine, and
rejoice that Thou hast vision so fair and so complete.
Rejoice that the Perfect Whole is so completely reflected
through Thee.

*My light has come.*

### SEEING THE PERFECT

My eyes behold the complete and perfect in all Creation,
"In all, over all and through all."
I see the perfect; there is nothing else to see, and no
suggestion of otherness can enter my thought.
I know only the perfect and the complete.
I am perfect and whole, now.

*I see the Good.*

### THE CIRCLE IS COMPLETE

The Circle of Love is complete.
It comprehends all, includes all, and binds all together with
cords of Everlasting Unity.
I cannot depart from Its Presence nor wander from Its care.

My Love is complete within me.

The Love of God binds me to Itself, and will not let me go.

I shall make a home for you, O my wonderful Love, and we
    shall journey through life hand in hand.

I shall sit in your Presence and learn the wondrous things
    You will tell me;

For You are God.

*Love sits within me.*


## THE THINGS THAT ARE

The things that are, were and evermore shall be.

Time, chance and change begone from my thought!

The Changeless is here to stay, and the Timeless cannot cease
    from Being.

The things that are shall remain, though heaven and earth
    should pass away.

I rest secure and safe within the Life of Endless Perfection
    and Completion.

My whole Being responds to the Realization of the Complete
    Whole.

*I am that which Is.*


## A SONG OF HOPE

My Life is in Thee, O Inner Presence.

I look upon Thee and hope springs forth into realization.

O Hope within me, undying evidence of Good,

Thou dost completely hold me in Thy loving embrace,
And from this fond caress assurance shall be born, and
confidence and love.

*My hope is in Thee.*

## BE STILL AND KNOW

"Be still and know that I am God."

I am still in Thy Presence.

I am quiet and peaceful, for I put my trust in Thee.

A great stillness steals over me and a great calm quiets my
whole being, as I realize Thy Presence.

The heart knows of Thee, O Most High within.

It is still in Thy Presence, and it puts its whole confidence in
Thee alone.

*In Thy Presence I am still.*

## CAST ASIDE ALL DOUBT

Cast aside all doubt, O Soul of mine, and be unafraid, for
Thy power is from On High.

He Who sitteth in the heavens shall be Thy
champion;

Thou need not fear; Come forth, O Spirit, from within and
express Thyself through me and let not my doubts hinder
Thy approach.

My faith shall go forth to meet Thee, and my confidence
shall embrace Thee.

My waiting thought shall bid Thee welcome to my house
of Love,
And Joy shall accompany us through the ages yet to come.
*I lay aside all fear and doubt.*


## DIVINE COMPANIONSHIP

I have an Inner Friend who walks and talks with me daily.
He is not afar off, but is within me, a constant companion.
I shall never become lonely, for my Friend is always near.
I have but to speak and He answers.
Before ever my lips spoke He told me of His love.
O my kind Friend, how dear to me is Thy presence.
*The Spirit within me is my Friend.*


## HIS EYE IS ON THE SPARROW

"His eye is on the sparrow and I know He watches me."
This is a blessed thought, for it means that we cannot
wander from His Presence, nor depart from His care.
Always He will watch over us and comfort us.
Forever we shall sit in His house and ceaselessly He will care
for us.
The All-Seeing Eye cannot overlook any one, and all, all shall
be kept in His care.
*All are kept in His care.*

## HOPE CANNOT DIE

Hope cannot die. Eternal Hope is forever warm and fresh
within me; the deathless Hope built upon the rock of
sure knowledge.

O Hope Sublime, O Life Supreme, behold I come to Thee as
a tired child, and Thou dost rekindle within me the fires
of Faith.

Strong, swift and sure, Faith springs forth into action and
my entire Being rises to meet the Dawn.

*Hope, Faith and Love are in me.*


## I AM NOT ALONE

I am not alone, for a Presence goes with me and daily
accompanies me on my travels.

Always I shall find this Divine Companion with me.

He will not desert nor allow me to go alone.

He will always be with me and near me, and will always
provide for every want.

*My life is hid with Christ in God.*


## I WENT INTO A MOUNTAIN

I have discovered a Secret Place within, where the thought
goes into a mountain high above the din of the world.

I have found in this mountain a Place of Peace and rest,

A Place of joy and comfort to the heart.

I have found that the Secret Place of God is within my own Soul.

*I will listen for Thy Voice.*


## THE JOY OF THE SOUL

My Soul within me rejoices at the realization of Life.

I am made glad as I behold my inner Light;

I cannot be sad nor depressed, for the All Good has claimed
me as Its own.

O Soul within me, rejoice and become glad, for Thy Light
has come and Thy Day of Salvation is at hand.

Be still within me and behold Him Who sitteth On High.

*I rejoice in my Life within me.*


## FREEDOM FROM SIN

I am free from belief in sin; there is neither sin nor sinner.

There is no judgment against anyone.

God does not condemn and man cannot.

All fear of sin is removed from me; all belief in punishment
is gone from me.

I live by the One Power, and no thought can enter to
disturb me.

*There is neither sin nor sinner.*


## FREE FROM SENSITIVENESS

My feelings cannot be hurt.

No one wishes to harm me, and there is nothing in me that

can believe in any separation from the All Good.

I perceive that I am free from all people, and I cannot be harmed nor mistreated.

I have such a sense of unity with all that the circle is complete and perfect.

I love my friends and they love me, and that love is in, and of, God, and cannot be marred nor hindered.

*I am filled with joy and love, forever.*

## I KEEP THE PROMISE

I shall keep the promise that I have made to myself.

I shall never again tell myself that I am poor, sick, weak nor unhappy.

I shall not lie to myself any more, but shall daily speak the truth to my inner Soul, telling It that It is wonderful and marvelous; that It is One with the Great Cause of all Life, Truth, Power and Action.

I shall whisper these things into my Soul until it breaks forth into songs of joy with the realization of Its Limitless possibilities.

*I shall assure my Soul.*

## LOVE GLEAMS THROUGH THE MIST

Through the mist of human fear love gleams and points the way to freedom.

I now decree and declare that I am free from all sense of bondage.

I am made perfect and whole through knowledge of the Real
    Life within me.

No illusions can enter my thought.

I know that there is One Power, and I know that this Power
    now protects me from all harm.

As Perfect Love casts out all fear, so my fear flees before the
    knowledge of Truth.

*I am not afraid.*

## No Bondage

There is no bondage nor limitation.

Every part of me moves in perfect harmony and freedom.

I cannot be tied, bound nor made inactive, for

I am Free Spirit, and the Power of my Life is from on High.

There is no inaction nor false action,

And I am now completely Free.

*I am free.*

## No Condemnation

There is no condemnation in me nor operating through me.

I am free from the belief or thought of men.

I walk my own way, immune to all suggestion of
    condemnation.

Only those thoughts can enter my mentality which I allow to
    enter.

I do not, and cannot, receive adverse thoughts.

Only those thoughts which are helpful and life-giving can
 find entrance to my house.

*There is no condemnation.*

## No False Habit

There are no vicious nor false habits.

Every desire of my thought and heart is satisfied in the Truth.

I do not long for anything nor feel the lack of anything.

I am complete within myself; I am perfect within myself;
 I am happy and satisfied within myself.

I am One with All Life within me.

*I am free.*

## No Hypnotism nor False Suggestion

There is no hypnotism nor false suggestion.

I represent the One Mind which cannot act against Itself nor
 can It act against me.

I am immune to all suggestion and cannot receive false
 thoughts, nor harbor them.

I am surrounded with a circle of Love and Protection.

Asleep or awake, I am free from false thoughts.

I see the nothingness of all belief in, or fear of, otherness;
 and I know that The One and Only Mind, alone, can act.

*Only the Good can enter.*

## No Mistakes

There are no mistakes; none have ever been made and none
ever will be made.

Nothing ever happened in the past to hinder or hurt.

There is no past, and I know, and can see, that there is no
belief in any past to rise against me.

I live in the Now, free from any yesterdays or tomorrows.

Now, I am Happy, Free and Complete.

*There are no mistakes.*


## There Are No Responsibilities

The Spirit has no responsibilities.

The Spirit knows no want nor fear.

It is complete within Itself, and lives by virtue of Its
own Being.

I am Spirit and cannot take on the fears of the world.

My ways are made straight before me.

The pathway of Life is an endless road of Eternal Satisfaction
and Perfect Joy.

My Life within me is Complete and Perfect, and has no cares
nor burdens.

It is Free Spirit and cannot be bound.

I rejoice in that Freedom.

*I rejoice in freedom.*

## THE TIME HAS COME

The time has come, the hour has struck.

The power from within has come forth and is expressing
through my word.

I do not have to wait; today is the time.

Today I enter into all Truth; today I am completely
healed.

Today I enter into my inheritance.

*Today the Truth has made me free.*


## WITHIN THY LAW IS FREEDOM

O, My Soul within me, Great is Thy Presence

Within Thy Law is freedom to all who will believe.

I believe in Thy Law and I love Thy precepts.

I know that Thy Law is perfect and It is a delight to my
Soul, for It is illumined with Thy Words of Power.

Thy Law is complete freedom to me, and to all for whom it
shall be spoken.

I speak the Word of freedom to all, and all shall receive it.

*I am free in Thy Law.*


## BEAUTY

I behold the Beautiful and the Pleasant.

My eyes see only that which is beautiful to look upon.

I will not see anything else nor believe in anything else.

I know that beauty has entered into my life, and will always
remain there.

*I see only the beautiful.*

## FRIENDSHIP OF THE SPIRIT AND OF MAN

The Friendship of the Spirit and of man is mine now and
forever.

Even now I see the countless numbers of friends coming and
going around me.

I enter into this friendship and this companionship with
gladness and rejoicing.

*I receive my friends.*

## I SERVE

I serve the world.

I wait upon the Lord within all men;

I call forth glory from On High through the minds of all
people.

I obey the will of Him Who inhabits Eternity.

I do the works of Him Who dwelleth among the heavens.

My Lord within commands and I obey.

*I do good to all people.*

## I SHALL NOT DOUBT NOR FEAR

I shall not doubt nor fear, for my salvation is from On High,
and the day of its appearing is now at hand.

I shall not doubt nor fear, for my whole being responds to
   the realization of Life within and around me.
I shall not fear, for the Hosts of Heaven are waiting upon me,
   and the Law of the Universe is my Salvation.
*I shall not fear.*


## I WAS TOLD TO LIVE

By some inner mystic Presence,
I was told to live and to love, to laugh and to be glad.
I was told to be still and know of the One Almighty Power, in
   and through all.
I was told to let that Power work through and in me.
I believed that voice and I received my Good.
*I am healed—The joy of Life.*


## LAW

I meditate upon the Law of God.
It is a Perfect Law and is now working for me and in and
   through me.
"The Law of the Lord is perfect."
I speak into that Law and it is done unto me.
*Thy Law is in my heart.*


## LOVE

The Love of the All Good is within me and through me.
That Love goes out to meet all who come into my atmosphere.

It radiates to all and is flowing through all.
My Love within me is Perfect.

> *Thy Love within me is Perfect.*

## LOVE DISSOLVES ALL FEAR

Greater than fear is Love.

Love dissolves all fear, casts out all doubt and sets the
captive free.

Love, like the River of Life, flows through me and refreshes
me with its eternal blessings.

Love cannot be afraid; it is fearless and strong, and is mighty
in its works.

It can accomplish all things through the Inner Light of that
faith in the All Good,

Which fills my very Being with a Powerful Presence.

> *Love casts out all fear.*

## MY AFFAIRS

My affairs are in the hands of Him
Who guides the planets in their course,
And Who causes the Sun to shine.
Divine Understanding attends me on the Way,
And I shall not be hindered in my work.
My affairs are controlled by Perfect Intelligence,
And cannot be hindered from expression.
I know that all that I do is done from the One Motive:

To express Life; and Life will be expressed
In and through me. I cannot hinder it.
*I am controlled by Intelligence.*

## MY BUSINESS

My business is directed by Divine Intelligence.
The All-Knowing Mind knows what to do and how to do it.
I do not hinder, but let It operate in my affairs.
It prospers and directs me and controls my life.
My affairs are managed by Love, and directed by
Wisdom, and they cannot fail to prosper and expand.
*My affairs are in His hands.*

## MY PROFESSION

My profession is the Activity of the Great Mind working
    through me.
As such It is a Divine Activity and is constantly in touch with
    Reality.
I am inspired in my work from On High with lofty ideals,
And my thought is illumined by the All-Knowing One.
*I am inspired.*

## NO DELAYS

There are no delays in the Divine Plan for me.
Nothing can hinder the operation of this Law unto my Life
    and Action.

Obstructions are removed from my path, and
I now enter into the realization and manifestation of
   complete fulfillment.
I do not have to wait, for the Law waits upon me at every
   turn in Life's road.

*Now it is done unto me.*

## NO MISREPRESENTATIONS

No one can misdirect; none can mislead me.
I am free from the belief in all lies and untruths;
I know and speak only the Truth, and the Truth alone can be
   spoken to me.
I know the false and can understand the Real.
I cannot be fooled nor misled; I am guided by Truth alone.

*There is no lie nor liar.*

## NO OBSTRUCTIONS

There are no obstructions to Life's Path; no hindrance to
   man's endeavors.
Let my Word be the Law of elimination to all thought of
   hindrance or delay,
And let the thing that I speak come forth into manifestation
   at once.
I behold it and see that it is even now done, complete and
   perfect.

*I receive now.*

## No Over-Action nor Inaction

There is no over-action nor inaction in Divine Law, for
everything moves according to perfect harmony.

Every idea of my body functions in accordance with this Law
of Perfect Life.

I now perceive that the action within me is perfect, complete
and harmonious.

Peace be unto every part of me, and perfect Life to every
member of my body.

I act in accordance with Divine Law.

*I am Perfect Life throughout my whole Being.*

## One with Perfect Action

I am One with Perfect Action. Everything that I do, say or
think is quickened into action through this right
understanding and this correct knowing.

The harmonious action of the Great Whole operates
through me now and at all times.

I am carried along by this Right Action and am compelled to
do the right thing at the right time.

There is nothing in me that can hinder this action from
flowing through me.

*The action of God is the only action.*

### PEACE, POISE AND POWER

Peace, Poise and Power are within me, for they are the
witnesses of the Inner Spirit of all Truth, Love and
Wisdom.

I am at peace within me, and all about responds to that
Great Calm of the Inner Soul which knows its rightful
place in the All Good.

Power is born from within me and passes into my experience
without effort or labor.

I rest in Security and Peace, for the Inner Light shines forth
and illumines the way.

*I rest in Thee.*

### STILLNESS AND RECEPTIVITY

I am still and receptive to Life.

I let Life flow through me into all that I do, say or think.

I shall let my Life be what it is, and shall not worry nor
complain.

I am now entered into the Secret Place of the Soul where
complete quiet reigns supreme and where God talks
to me.

*I receive.*

### THANKSGIVING AND PRAISE

I will give thanks to my Inner Life for all Its Marvelous
Wonders, and for all Its Wonderful Works.

I will sing and be glad, for I know that I am hidden with
Truth in a Perfect Life.

*The fullness of Joy is mine.*

## THE INNER LIGHT

The Light of Heaven shines through me and illumines my
path.

The Light Eternal is my guide and my protection.

In that Light there is no darkness at all.

It is a Perfect Light shining from the altar of a perfect
Love.

O Light and Love within me, Thou art welcome.

*Light shines through me and illumines the Way.*

## THE NIGHT IS FILLED WITH PEACE

I wrap myself in the mantle of Love and fall asleep, filled
with Peace.

Through the long night Peace remains with me, and at the
breaking of the new day I shall still be filled with Life
and Love.

I shall go forth into the new day confident and happy.

*I rest in Thee.*

## THE SEAL OF APPROVAL

The Seal of Approval is upon me, and I am not condemned
by the thought or the act of man.

I will fear no evil, for I know that the Great Judge of all
    controls my every act.
Let every fear of man be removed from me and let the
    Silence of my soul bear witness to the Truth.
*God approves of me.*


## THE SECRET WAY

There is a Secret Way of the Soul which all may know.
It is the Way of Peace and Love.
This Secret Way leads into places of joy
And into the house of good.
It is the Way of the Spirit, and all may enter
    who will.
I tread the Secret Way of good, the Path of Peace,
And I enter into "The Secret Place of The Most High."
*The Secret Place of The Most High is within me.*


## THE SHINING PATH

The Pathway of Life shines before me unto the Perfect Day.
I walk the pathway of the Soul to the Gate of Good.
I enter into the fulfillment of my desires.
Nothing need be added to and nothing can be taken from the
    All Good which is forever expressing Itself in me.
Daily shall I receive Its great blessings and my Soul shall
    rejoice forevermore.
*I am now entered into my good.*

### THE THINGS I NEED COME TO ME

Whatever I need comes to me from the All Good.

Divine Intelligence working through me always knows

    just what I need and always supplies it when I need it.

This Law is unfailing and sure, and cannot be broken.

I receive my Good daily as I go along the pathway of Life,

    and I cannot be robbed of my birthright to freedom and

    happiness.

I receive my Good.

### THE WAY IS MADE CLEAR BEFORE ME

The Way is made clear before me; I do not falter nor fall.

The Way of the Spirit is my Way, and I am compelled to walk

    in it.

My feet are kept on the Path of Perfect Life.

The Way is prepared before me, and that Way is a Path of

    Peace, of Fulfillment and Joy.

The Way is bright with the light of Love and Kindness.

The Way I tread is a pleasant and a happy one.

I see the Way and I walk in It.

### AS LOVE ENTERS, FEAR DEPARTS

As Love enters, fear vanishes.

I am so filled with Love that no fear can enter my thought.

I am not afraid, for I know that a Perfect Intelligence guards

    and governs my every act.

Perfect Love casteth out all fear.

I am unafraid, and strong in my faith in that inner Presence
that keeps me from all harm.

*Perfect Love casteth out all fear.*

### INFINITE LIFE WITHIN

Infinite Life within me, which is God, guard Thou my feet
and keep Thou my way.

Let me not stray from Thee, but compel me to do
Thy will.

I am guarded and governed by an Infinite Intelligence and
an Omnipotent Power.

No mistakes can be made and none ever have been made.

An unerring judgment operates through me and I am led by
the Spirit of Truth into all Good and into all Peace and
Happiness.

*Infinite Life within me.*

### MY FEET SHALL NOT FALTER

My feet shall not falter, for they are kept upon the path of
Life through the Power of the Eternal Spirit.

This Spirit is my spirit now.

Guide Thou my feet; compel my way; direct my paths and
keep me in Thy Presence.

My feet are guarded and I am guided into The All Good.

*He guides my feet.*

## NO HARM SHALL BEFALL YOU

No harm shall befall you, my friend, for a Divine
Presence attends your way and guards you into The
All Good.
Loving kindness awaits you at every turn of Life's road.
Guidance is yours along the pathway of experience,
And an Infallible Power protects you.
God, Himself, and no other is your Keeper.

*I proclaim this for you.*

## POWER TO LIVE

I have the power to live the life of good.
My power is from On High, it cannot be taken from me;
It will not leave me desolate.
Power flows through me and is in me, and
I can now feel and sense it.
The Power to live is in me and it cannot desert me.
It is my power and is continually present.

*I am the power to live.*

## THE CIRCLE OF LOVE

A circle of love is drawn around me and mine, and all.
No harm can enter that Sacred Circle, for it is the Love of
God.
It is a complete protection from all evil.
"I will fear no evil, for Thou art with me."

There is no evil and no harm.

I am free from all sense of fear.

*Love surrounds and protects me.*


## THE CIRCLE OF PROTECTION

I draw around me a circle of love and protection.

No harm can enter nor find place within that charmed circle
of life and love, for it represents God's Loving Care and
Eternal Watchfulness.

I will rest within me now, and I will speak comfort to my
Soul and tell It of all the wonders of Its life, safe from the
din of strife and fear.

*I am protected from On High.*


## THE POWER WITHIN BLESSES ALL

The Power within me is blessing all mankind, and is forever
healing all with whom I come in contact.

The Power within me is God, and It must bless and help and
heal all who come near It.

Silently the work goes on, and silently all are being helped by
this Inner Power which is operating through me.

I will give thanks that my Power within is silently blessing and
helping every one to whom my thought reaches.

*The Life within me blesses all mankind.*

222

### THE QUICK ANSWER

My answer comes quickly and surely back to me from On High.
My answer will not fail me, for the Law of the Universe is the Power through which it comes.
I shall not doubt nor fear, for the answer is swift and certain.

*My answer comes.*

### A SONG OF JOY

There is a Song upon my lips today; it sings of the glad heart and the happy ways of Life.
I will listen to my song, for it carols to me the glad tidings of Great Joy, of Love and Life.
It tells me of the Wondrous Journey of the Soul and the Boundless Life in which my life is hid.

*I am filled with joy.*

### BORN OF ETERNAL DAY

Child of All Good, you are born of Eternal Day.
There is no evening of the Soul, for it shall live forever.
It is Deathless and Perfect, Complete and One with the Everlasting.
No thought of tomorrow can disturb the calm of him who knows that Life is one Eternal Day.
No fear can enter where Love reigns, and Reason keeps faith with Hope.

The thoughts of the tomorrows and the yesterdays are
swallowed up in the great realization of the Perfect Here
and the Complete Now.

*Today I completely accept my wholeness.*


## I Arise and Go Forth

I arise and go forth into the Dawn of the New Day, filled
with faith and assurance in the All Good.

I arise, I arise, I sing with joy!

I proclaim the One Life: "In all and through all."

I arise, I arise, I shout with gladness that is within me.

I declare this day to be Complete, Perfect and Eternal.

*I respond to Life.*


## Inspiration

Come, Thou Great and Infinite Mind and inspire me to do
great deeds.

Acquaint me with Thy knowledge and in Thy wisdom make
me wise.

I would be taught of Thee, Inner Light, and inspired by Thy
presence.

I will listen for Thy Voice and it will tell me of great things to
be done.

I will walk in Thy Paths and they will lead me into All Good.

I will be inspired from On High.

O Wonderful Presence, flooding me, filling me with Thy
Light, Thou dost inspire me!
*I feel the inspiration of Spirit.*

### THE DAWN HAS COME

Out of the darkness of the long night the Dawn has come.

I rise to meet the new day, filled with confidence and
strength.

I arise and go forth into the dawn, inspired and refreshed by
the Living Spirit within me.

O Day, you shall never die; the sun shall never set upon your
perfect glory.

For the Lamp of the Soul has been re-kindled with the oil of
Faith,

And Love has cleansed the windows of Life with the spirit of
gladness.

They shall nevermore grow dim with fear, for Perfect Love
casteth out all fear.

I am renewed in strength through knowing Good.
*My light has come.*

### COMPLETE CONFIDENCE

My confidence in the All Good is complete.

My faith in the Power of Spirit is supreme.

I have no doubts nor uncertainties.

I know that my Good is at hand, and
I realize that no fear can hinder
That Good from making Its appearance in my life and affairs.
I know that my Life and Good are complete.
Evil cannot touch nor hinder my work.
I rest in security, for
THE ONE MIND IS MY COMPLETE REFUGE AND
     STRENGTH.

*I am serene and confident.*


### DRAWING THE GOOD

I draw my Good to me as I travel along the Way of Life, and
     nothing can keep It from me.
My Good will always follow me.
I accept the Good and rejoice that it is with me.

*I accept the Good.*


### I FEAR NO EVIL

"I will fear no evil, for Thou art with me."
I will not be afraid, for the All Good is constantly with me
     and is always near at hand to guide and comfort.
There is no evil in the Truth, and no power of darkness to
     hinder the Light from shining.
I will not be afraid, for there is One within Who protects and
     keeps me from all harm.

*I fear no evil.*

### I Have Known, Always

I have always known the Truth, and no fear can keep my
inner knowledge from me.

My wisdom from within comes forth into daily expression.

Knowledge from On High is given to me, and I shall always
be led of the Spirit.

*I know the Truth.*

### I Meet My Good

Today I meet my Good; it knows me and will not let me
depart from it.

My Good is at hand, and I cannot be robbed of it.

Good is forever expressing itself to me and mine.

I can even now see and hear and feel the All Good in and
around me.

It presses itself against me, and fills me with a great surge
of Life.

*My Good is at hand.*

### My Atmosphere

My atmosphere is attracting the Good; it is constantly on the
alert to see and know the Good, and to bring it into my
experience.

There is that within me that calls forth abundance and
happiness from Life. I am surrounded with an
atmosphere of Peace, Poise and Power.

All who come in contact with that great Calm of my
Life are made strong and confident, are healed and
blessed.
"Bless the Lord, O my Soul, and all that is within me, bless
His Holy Name."
*I am hid with Christ in God.*


## MY GOOD IS COMPLETE
My Good is complete; it is finished; it is now here and is
conscious of me and of mine.
I do not have to wait for my Good; it is at hand and ever
ready to spring forth and express itself to me.
I accept my Good and gladly acknowledge it to be my daily
companion.
My Good is mine now, and I can see it and feel it and
know it.
*Today I claim my Good.*


## MY OWN SHALL COME TO ME
From far and near my own shall come to me. Even now it is
coming to me and I receive it.
My own is now manifesting itself to me, and I see and
know its presence. My own shall know and respond
to me.

My own cannot be kept from me, neither can I keep my
good away from me. I receive my good NOW.

My own shall find me. No matter where I go, it will follow
and claim me.

I cannot hide myself from my own.

My own shall come to me, even though I deny it; for there is
nothing in me that can hinder it from entering and
taking possession of my Soul.

*My own is now expressed.*

## MY SOUL REFLECTS THY LIFE

My Soul reflects Thy Life and rejoices in the happy thought
that it looks on Thee alone.

O Soul of mine, look out and up and on; and reflect to me
the wondrous Life of The All Good.

Look thou upon The One, and be saved.

Behold thou His Face forevermore.

*My Soul reflects Thy Life.*

## SORROW FLEES FROM ME

As the Great Joy of Life comes into my Soul, flooding me
with Its wondrous light, all sorrow and sadness flee
from me.

I shall not grieve, for nothing is lost nor gone from me.

My own cannot be kept from me.

My own knows me and will follow me wherever I go.

I am filled with the Joy of living and the Great Peace that
comes to all who believe.

*I am made glad forevermore.*

## SUBSTANCE AND SUPPLY

The Substance of the Spirit is my Daily Supply.

I cannot be without my Good.

I can see that the constant stream of Life, flowing to
me, brings into my experience all that makes Life happy
and worthwhile.

I rest in security, knowing that Infinite Good is within and is
expressing through me.

*I receive my good.*

## THE EVER AND THE ALL

Life always was and evermore shall be, "World without end."

All the Power there is, is mine now.

All the Life, Truth and Love of the Universe is now and
forever Flowing through my Soul.

The All Good cannot change.

I shall always have access to my Eternal God within me.

*I am Changeless Life within me.*

### THE HOUSE OF LOVE

I dwell in the house of Love;

My dwelling place is filled with peace and eternal calm.

Love attends me in my home of the Soul, and

Joy awaits upon me in "The Secret Place of The Most High."

My house is built for me by the hand of Love, and

I shall never leave this Home of the Spirit, for it is always

    present.

I shall abide in this home forevermore.

        *My house is a house of love.*

### ARISE, MY SPIRIT

Arise, my Spirit, arise and shine.

Let Thy light illumine my path, and let Thy wisdom direct

    my way.

Compel my will to do Thy bidding, and command my Soul

    to look to Thee.

I will follow Thee, my Spirit, and learn of Thee.

I will sit in the Silence and listen and watch, and

I will see Thy light and hear Thy voice.

I will follow Thee and will not depart from Thee,

For in Thee alone is Peace.

        *Arise and shine.*

### COMMAND MY SOUL

Spirit within me, command my Soul to do Thy bidding;

Compel me to follow the course of Truth and Wisdom.

Control my inward thoughts and my outward ways,

And make me to understand Thy Laws.

Command my Soul to turn to Thee for guidance and
    light;

To turn to Thee for wisdom and knowledge.

Let the paths of my Life be made straight and sure;

Let the Journey of my Soul find its completion in Thee.

*Command my Soul to do Thy bidding.*


### DESPAIR GIVES WAY TO JOY

Despair gives way to joy at the thought of Thee, Indwelling
    Good.

I cannot be sad when I think of Thee.

My sorrow is turned to gladness and my shame to rejoicing.

My tears are wiped away and the sunlight of the Spirit shines
    through the clouds of depression and lights the way to
    Heaven.

*Thy Joy has made me glad.*


### FREE SPIRIT WITHIN ME

Free Spirit within me, Unbound and Perfect, teach me
    Thy ways and make known to me Thy Limitless
    Completion.

O Spirit of Life, control my every action and thought.

Compel me to follow Thy light that I too may be free and
complete.

I will follow Thy footsteps and learn of Thee all the
wondrous secrets of Life.

I will follow Thy Light into the Perfect Day.

*Free Spirit within me.*

### FULLNESS OF LIGHT

The Light of Life is full within me and around me.

It shines forth into the Perfect Day.

O Light within, lighting my path to peace,

I adore and love You and I let You shine.

Go forth and bless all who come to You, Light within.

My Light radiates to all and through all.

*My Light has come.*

### HE WHO INHABITS ETERNITY

He Who inhabits Eternity keeps watch over me and mine.

"He Who neither slumbers nor sleeps" forever keeps watch
over all.

I will rest in the assurance of Love and Protection.

O Thou Great Overshadowing Presence,

I am conscious of Thy care; I am aware of Thy loving kindness.

I rest in Thee.

*Be still and know.*

## I Listen

I will listen for Thy voice, Inner Presence.

It will guide me and acquaint me with all knowledge.

Thy voice is sweet and tender; it is always kind and gentle.

O Lover of my Soul, how I adore Thee! How I love Thee!

How I love Thy voice; it thrills me with gladness and joy.

It fills me with peace and calm, and it soothes me.

It quiets me and gives me wonderful rest.

I listen, O Divine Speaker, I listen to Thee alone.

*I listen for Thy voice.*


## Joy Has Come to Live with Me

Joy has come to live with me. How can I be sad?

I do so love Thy presence, which is joy within me.

It makes me glad and I sing, for I am so filled with

Thy Spirit that I cannot be depressed nor unhappy.

I am filled with the joy of the Spirit, and I overflow with the

gladness of life.

Thou art a Happy Companion to travel with me through

Life;

Wonderful Joy, Thou art so radiant and beaming,

It is impossible to be sad in Thy presence.

I shall give myself to Thee and remain with Thee, for Thou

art complete and satisfying.

I find fulfillment in Thee, and joy forevermore.

*I am filled with the Spirit of Joy.*

## MY THOUGHT IS IN THEE

My thought is in Thee, Inner Light.

My words are from Thee, Inner Wisdom.

My understanding is of Thee, Inner God.

I cannot be hid from Thee, my inspiration and my life.

*My thought is in Thee.*

## O LOVE DIVINE

O Love Divine within me, I am overpowered by Thy Presence.

I am speechless, for words cannot utter the things that Thou
    hast revealed to me.

Why dost Thou love me so, and why clasp me so close to Thy
    Eternal Heart?

O Blessed Presence, I know, for Thou hast claimed me as
    Thine own.

I shall nevermore walk apart from Thee.

*The love of God is within me.*

## PEACE STEALS THROUGH THE SOUL

Peace steals through the waiting Soul, and the comfort of the
    Spirit comes into the stillness of the heart.

Peace, like an ocean of Infinite Life, reflects itself through me
    and calms every turbulent feeling.

I am at peace and rest in the knowledge of the All Good
    which is at hand.

*I rest in peace.*

## STAND FORTH AND SPEAK

Stand forth and speak, Spirit within me.

Proclaim Thy presence, announce Thy course.

Declare through me Thy wondrous works and

Let the children of men hear Thy voice.

Behold, He maketh all things new.

The Spirit within speaks words of Truth and Life to all.

The Spirit within me is God.

*I speak the Truth.*

## SUBTLE ESSENCE OF SPIRIT WITHIN ME

Subtle Essence of Spirit within me, flowing through me;

Elixir of Life in my veins purifying me with Thy marvelous
Life,

I let Thy Spirit cleanse me from all false thought and idea;

I let Thy Life flow through me in a complete and Perfect
Whole.

*I feel the presence of Spirit within me.*

## THE EVERLASTING ARMS

His Arms enfold me, His Strength upholds me,

His Presence fills me with Life and Joy.

I shall nevermore be sad nor depressed, for I know that I do
not walk Life's path alone.

There is One Who goes with me and tells me all the things
that I should know.

There is a Presence with me guiding me into the Perfect Way.
*I rejoice in knowing that I am not alone.*

## THE MANTLE OF LOVE

Like a cloak His Love is wrapped around me. Like a warm
garment, It shelters me from the storms of life.
I feel and know that an Almighty Love envelops me in Its
close embrace.
O Love Divine, My Love, how wonderful Thou art. I am
open to receive Thy great blessing.
*Love envelops me.*

## THE VOICE OF TRUTH

The Voice of Truth speaks to me and through me.
The Voice of Truth guides me and keeps me on the Path of
the Perfect Day.
I will listen to the Inner Voice and It will tell me what to do
in the hour of need.
I shall be told everything that I ought to know when
the time of need arrives, and I shall not be misled.
The Voice of Truth cannot lie, but always speaks to me from
On High.
Nothing enters but This Voice, for it is the Voice of God.
*God speaks to me.*

### THE WITNESS OF TRUTH

There is a Witness within me who knows the Truth and who
    will not let me enter into falsehood.

My Inner Guide keeps me on the Pathway of Life
    and directs me at all times to that which is right
    and best.

I shall never be without this witness of the Spirit, for I
    believe in It and accept It as the Great Companion of
    the Soul.

*The spirit within me is perfect now.*

### THROUGH THE LONG NIGHT WATCHES

Through the long night watches Thou hast been with me.

In the dark places of human ignorance Thy hand hath
    guided me,

Thy light hath lighted the pathway of desolation to a land of
    plenty.

I have perceived Thee from afar, and my soul hath yearned to
    Thee, O Thou Mighty One!

The Spirit within me hath urged me on to the goal, and I
    have not been misled.

I have been guided and guarded through the long journey,
    and Thy Presence hath been made known to me.

I awake from the dream and reënter the house of my
    Lord clothed with Peace and robed in colors of Light.

*The Spirit of Truth watches over me.*

### THY STRENGTH IS SUFFICIENT

O Spirit of man and God within me, Thy Power is great, and
  Thy Knowledge goes beyond the range of human
  experience.

Thy Wisdom excels that of all else, and beside Thee there is
  none other.

In Thy Strength do I daily walk and live;

In Thy Presence do I always rest in peace and joy.

Spirit within me and without, Powerful Thou art, and Great;

Wonderful is Thy Might, and Complete is Thy Understanding.

I let Thy Mighty Strength flow through me,

And out into all the paths of my human endeavors.

*Life from within expresses through me.*


### WAITING ON THEE

In waiting on Thee there is fullness of Life.

I wait on Thee, my Inner Lord; I listen for Thy voice.

I hear Thy word; I do Thy will; again I wait on Thee.

And listening, I hear Thee say: "Be perfect, be complete; live,
  love, be glad."

*Sit thou in the stillness and let thy Lord speak.*


### WHOSE RIGHT IT IS TO COME

He has come Whose right it is.

He has made His home within me, and will nevermore
  depart from me.

I shall walk no more alone, for One walks with me
Who knows the path of Life, and Whose feet will never falter
    nor fail.
My Inner Light shines through the mist of human beliefs
And frees me from the bondage of fear and limitation.
I shall walk with You, my Friend, and shall learn of You the
    ways of Life and Freedom.
We shall travel together from this day, and none can part us,
For we are united in the perfect bonds of an everlasting unity.

*I walk with Thee.*

### I CONTROL MY MENTAL HOUSEHOLD

I conquer my mental household and cast out all fear and
    doubt.
Let my Word cast out all sense of fear and doubt and let my
    thoughts be lifted unto Him Who lives Within.
My Word has dissolved all fear within me, and has cast out
    all doubt.
My Word shall guard my thought and make me receive only
    that which is Good and Perfect.

*I control my life.*

### MY WORD COMES BACK TO ME

My word comes back to me laden with the fruits of its own
    speech.

My word is the Law unto my Life, and the Law unto
    everything that I speak.

O Word, go forth and heal and bless all humanity.

Tell them of their Divine Birthright.

Tell the stranger that he is not alone, but that One goes
    with him

Who knows and cares.

Tell the sick that they are healed and the poor that they
    cannot want,

Tell the unhappy of the joy of the Soul, and break the bonds
    of those who are in prison.

    *My word shall come back to me blessed of God and man.*

## MY WORD SHALL BEAR FRUIT

The Word of my mouth shall bear fruit.

It shall accomplish and prosper, and shall not return unto
    me void.

My Word is the law unto the thing whereunto it is sent, and
    it cannot come back empty-handed.

I send out my Word and it is the law unto my life.

My Word is the Law unto the thing whereunto it is spoken,
    and will become fulfilled in the right way and at the right
    time.

My Word is complete and perfect, and is the Presence and
    then Power of the One Mind that is in and through all.

I speak the Word and know that it will accomplish.

I wait in perfect confidence for the Word to fulfill itself in
my life.

*My Word Is Law.*

## O Man, Speak Forth Thy Word

O man, speak forth thy word and be not afraid.

Did you not know? have you not heard?

His Divinity is planted within thee, and thy word is one with
all power.

The Spirit of the Most High is thy Spirit, and the Word of
God is thy word.

Thy freedom is hid within thee, and thy inner light shall
illumine thy way.

Speak man, and be free! Announce and proclaim thy works!

Let thy word go forth with power, and thy Spirit shall
conquer all.

*Spirit within me, speak.*

## The Power of the Word

The Word is a mighty Power, and that Word is in me and
through me now.

My Word is one with the All Good and cannot fail to
accomplish the desired ends.

My Word goes forth with Power unto everything that I do,
say or think.

The Word is my Power by day and by night.

I will speak that Word and trust in the great Law of Life to
fulfill it.

*I speak the word in full confidence.*

### THE WORD OF POWER

My Word is a Word of Power, for I know that it is the Word
of the Great God within me.

My Word shall accomplish and prosper, and shall do
good unto all who call upon my name.

My Word is a tower of strength and cannot be denied.

It is complete and perfect here and now.

My Word is the Word of God.

*My Word is the Word of God.*

### THE UNASSAILABLE TRUTH AND THE IRRESISTIBLE WORD

The Truth within me is unassailable, and the Power of the
Word is irresistible.

I can even now feel that my Word has gone forth with Power
and Reality, and that it will accomplish that purpose for
which it was created.

Limitless is its Power and wonderful are its works.

It can be nothing less than the Almighty working in and
through me.

I will let this Word of the Spirit go forth from my mouth,
and heal and bless the world.

It shall be as a strong tower unto all who call upon it.
The Truth is Complete and Perfect, and is within
    me now.
        *My Word is complete and perfect, now.*


### I Behold in Thee His Image

I behold in thee His Image.
In thee, my friend, I see God, and through you I feel His
    presence.
I see in the hand that gives, His hand;
And in the voice that speaks of Love, I hear Him speak.
For His lines have gone out into all places,
And from the highest to the lowest, all, all partake of His
    nature.
"For He is all in all, over all and through all."
        *I perceive that God is in all people.*


### I See No Evil

I see no evil; I behold only the good.
I have seen the drunkard lying in the gutter, and the saint
    kneeling in ecstasy before the high altar of his faith; but I
    have found no difference.
I have perceived that each, in his own tongue, is seeking to
    express the One Life.
I will not separate and divide; I cannot condemn nor
    censure, for I know that there is but One in All.

I know that all came from the One, and all will return to
the One.

I know that all are now in the One, and that each is seeking
to express the One.

*I know and love all.*


## I SHALL NEVER DIE

I shall never die, for the Spirit within me is God and cannot
change.

My life is hid within the Universe of Love and Light, and that
Light shall live forever.

Go, fear of death and change; begone from my thought, fear
of death and uncertainty.

That which is cannot become that which is not; and that
which I am can never change.

The Spirit of Eternity is enthroned within me, and the
Life of Endless Ages flows through my being.

From Eternity to Eternity my Life flows along its way of
peace and harmony.

Time brings but more glory to crown me with its pleasures.

*My life is forever.*


## LOVE TO THE WORLD

My Love goes out to every one in the world;

I do not exclude anything, for I love all Nature and everything that is.

My Love warms and lightens everything that it touches, and
   it goes out into all places.
The Love flowing through me is a Power to all who
   come into contact with it, and all feel and know that
   I love.
Love within me is Complete and Perfect.

*Love within me is Complete.*


## MY LIFE IS ONE WITH GOD

My life is in God; it cannot be hurt nor hindered in its
   expression.
God lives and expresses through me; His work is complete
   and perfect in me now.
I know His life to be my life, and I know that my life is
   complete and perfect.

*My Life is in God.*


## NO MISUNDERSTANDINGS

There are no misunderstandings.
All is made clear between the ideas of Good.
No false sense of separation can come between people, nor
   disturb the realization of the Unity of All Life.
I perceive that I am one with all people, and all are One
   with me.
There is no separation.

*There is no separation.*

### THE DIVINE PLAN FOR ME

The Divine Plan for me is Perfect. I am held in the Mind of
God as a Complete and Perfect Expression of Life and
Truth.

No power can hinder nor mar this Inner Image of Reality,
for It is God-given and God-kept.

*God gave and God will keep.*

### THE PERSONALITY OF GOD

The Great Personality of God is my Personality; the Limitless
Knowingness of the Spirit is my Knowingness, and the
One Mind is my mind.

All, All live in One Infinite Being, and each manifests the
One Who is formed through and in all.

Man is the Personality of God in manifestation and cannot
be left without the Inner Witness of the Spirit.

I now realize that the Infinite Personalness of the Spirit is
my Personality, and I rejoice to know the Truth about
myself.

*God is my Personality.*

### THE RADIATION OF LIFE

The life of God within me radiates and shines forth from me
in a constant stream of Light to all.

The One Life flowing through me is Life to all who come
near.

The One Power operating through me is flowing into everything that I contact.

*Life radiates from me.*


## UNITY

Today I realize that I am One with the All Good; my God
and I are One.

I cannot be hid from His face.

I behold Thee, O Most High, enthroned in my temple of
flesh.

Thy secret place is within me. I feel Thy presence,

I hear Thy voice, I rejoice in Thy Light.

Today my body responds to the Divine Behest: "Be perfect."

I know of my perfection and wholeness; I am complete and
perfect now.

Let every thought of disease flee from me, and let Thy Light
shine.

O Light Eternal, O Light of my Life, I come into Thy
presence with joy and thanksgiving.

*So be it.*


## WITHIN THEE IS FULLNESS OF LIFE

Within Thee is fullness of Life.

Within Thee is complete Joy and everlasting Peace.

Within Thee is all.

Thou art in me as I am in Thee, and we are all in all.

My Life is full and complete within me, and that Life I give
    to all men freely;
And from all I receive again that which I have given,
For it is One in All.
        *I am One with the fullness of All life.*

### I Am Complete in Thee

Almighty God, Everlasting Good, Eternal Spirit, Maker of
    all things and Keeper of my Life, Thou art All.
Infinite Presence within, in Whom all live; Joy Supreme,
    flooding all with gladness, I adore Thee.
Eternal Peace, undisturbed and quiet, I feel Thy calm.
O Thou Who dost inhabit Eternity and dost dwell within all
    Creation, Who Dost live through all things and in all
    people, hear Thou my prayer.
I would enter Thy gates with joy and live at peace in Thy
    House.
I would find a resting place in Thee, and in Thy presence
    live.
Make me to do Thy will and from Thy wisdom teach me the
    ways of Truth.
Compel me to follow Thee and let me not pursue the paths
    of my own counsel.
O Eternal and Blessed Presence, illumine my mind and
    command my will that my Soul may be refreshed and
    that my life may be renewed.

As deep cries unto deep, so my thought cries unto Thee and
   Thou dost answer.

I am renewed and refreshed; my whole being responds to
   Thy love, and I am complete in Thee.

All my ways are guarded and guided, and I shall live with
   Thee eternally.

O Lover of my Soul and Keeper of my Spirit, none can
   separate us, for we are One.

So shall Thy Wisdom guide me, Thy Presence dwell within
   me, Thy Love keep me and Thy Life envelop me now and
   forevermore.

*I rest in Thee.*

# Meditations, Concluded

*The following meditations are printed just as they were given in class and group work.*

## A TREATMENT FOR ALCOHOLISM OR OTHER DRUG ADDICTION

There is but one Universal Life, God or Spirit. This Universal Life is a principle of perfect harmony and right action. It is an omnipresent and self-knowing principle, whole and complete within Itself. It is forever calm and peaceful. It is, therefore, a principle of complete satisfaction which knows no unsatisfied desire. The only appetite or desire of Infinite Mind is for the complete manifestation of Its own constructive contemplation.

My life is a part of this Universal Life; Its peace, calm and satisfaction are manifesting in and through me *now* in absolute perfection. My spirit, being one with Universal Spirit, has nothing to desire or long for—save the natural expression of peace, poise and complete satisfaction. That subjective race-thought, which speaks to me as limitation or a desire for abnormal stimulation, has no answering or recognizing voice within me. I turn from all such inharmonious thoughts toward the reality of my oneness with Universal Life (the Father) realizing here in the formless Realm of Reality, the complete satisfaction of knowingness, the sense of calm well-being, wisdom and understanding. Here within the Realm of Reality (the Kingdom of God) I sense the truth of my complete mastery over all *things*. My body is that concept of Universal Mind which is composed of the Creator's perfect ideas (God's body). Within the form, which is commonly termed the human body, is nothing which can speak to me, demanding anything whatsoever. I dwell within the Realm of the Universal and declare that the calm and complete satisfaction of the Self-Knowing God is expressing in and through me, unhindered and unopposed.

I go forth with a complete sense of mastery in the realm of form (my earth experience) unafraid, happy and joyous in my expression of all that is desirable and constructive; knowing that all destructive desires and inharmonious thoughts disappear and dissolve into the nothingness from which they came, having no power to perpetuate themselves, since they are neither person, place nor thing.

*I Do Know the Truth and I Am Free*

# A TREATMENT TO HEAL CONFUSION OR DISCORD

I know there is a Spirit in me which unfolds Itself to me; and I know that this Spirit—or Infinite Wisdom and Divine Love and Perfect Law—enlightens my consciousness and awakens within me, within the personal, the knowledge of Its meaning, the realization of Its Presence, and the power of Its Law. I am conscious that this Universal IT is an ever-present Being to me and to every man, because where the Universe personifies, It becomes personal. Therefore, there is within me an immediate Presence, the Infinite of the finite self, all-knowing, all-wise, and forever perfect. It is this Real Me that I seek to vision in my thought, that I seek to embody in my consciousness. It is that ME that cannot be sick, knows no lack, has no limitation, never suffered want, and cannot experience fear.

The Spirit of Infinite Peace is my spirit now. The Presence of That which is perfect is within me, in every function, in every organ, every attribute and every atom. In each cell, there vibrates the perfect Divine Wholeness.

And this comprehension, this application to myself, this knowingness, reveals me to myself and heals the apparent confusion and discomfort, because WHERE THAT PERFECT CIRCULATION IS *KNOWN*, IT IS ESTABLISHED! Where that perfect efficiency is known, it is demonstrated. THE TRUTH KNOWN IS IMMEDIATELY MANIFEST, and I am now conscious of my own wholeness, my own depth of being, the spiritual me, the Divine Self.

And now I know that my Divine Self is not separated from the self that appears; that the Universal Self is made manifest because the Word is made flesh and dwells in the midst of my physical me. The Word becomes activity and surrounds me with a harmonious activity—with happy action and perfect reaction. The Word becomes Light and guides me into all good. The Word becomes beauty and surrounds me with beauty. The Word, which is Substance, becomes supply and brings to me everything I need, because "The Word was with God and the Word was God," and the Word is God.

This consciousness of Wholeness, this recognition of the Self, obliterates every belief of confusion and discord from my life.

# I ACCEPT THE FULLNESS
# OF MY OWN DIVINE WELL-BEING

Within myself is that which is perfect, that which is complete, that which is divine; that which was never born and cannot die; that which lives, which is God—the Eternal Reality. Within myself is peace, poise, power, wholeness and happiness. All the power that there is and all the presence that there is, and all the life that there is, is God—the Living Spirit Almighty—and this Divine and Living Spirit is within me. It is Wholeness. It is never weary. It is never tired. It is Life. It is complete Peace. It is never afraid; It is never confused. It is always poised and peaceful. It is always in a state of perfect equilibrium.

This is the truth about *myself*; there is no other self. Every image of fear is erased from my mind, every sense of confusion leaves my thought. My mind now entertains and reflects the Divine into everything which I do, say and think—into my body, into my affairs. That Divine within me is Wholeness, and my mind reflects this Wholeness into every organ, every function, every action, every reaction of my physical being, renewing it after the Perfect Pattern—the Christ within me. Universal Substance reflects Itself, into my mind, into daily supply, so that everything I need each day is supplied. *Before the need, is the thing, and with the apparent need it is met.* There is Something within me which goes before me and prepares the way wherever I go—making straight the way, making perfect the way, making immediate and instant, and permanent and harmonious, every situation. Consequently, my mind reflects the fullness of that Divine Substance, which heals every sense of lack in my life. Peace, poise, power, perfection, Living Spirit within me, is me, myself.

*I Accept the Fullness of My Own Divine Well-Being*

# THE GIFTS OF GOD ARE MINE TODAY

It is the Father's good pleasure to give me the Kingdom of Heaven, or harmony and abundance. Today He opens to me the blessings of His infinite and eternal treasure, inviting me to dip deeply into it. As I believe in my heart, so it is done unto me in all things. As I ask, so do I receive, a full measure unto my faith, pressed down and running over.

These and other Divine promises and assurances sing in me; the Still Small Voice reminds me that all that the Father hath is mine. This day I listen deeply to that Still, Small Voice and believe Its promises.

I fear nothing—neither lack, limitation, disappointment nor distress of any kind, for is not the Father always with me? What caused the appearance of lack in my life? Simply my fear, or my belief that the Father could forsake me. I do not believe that now, and it no longer matters to me what is the appearance of today, or what has gone before. Today is new, and I am newly awakened in it, and I believe with dauntless faith that my good, in full measure, comes to me from God today.

I now believe that it is, indeed, the Father's good pleasure to give me of His bounty. I know that He gives as I ask, without question or limit, and I am ready to receive.

*The Gifts of God Are Mine Today*


## ABUNDANCE IS MY INHERITANCE

Abundance is mine. I cannot be deprived of my supply. The trees do not lack for leaves, nor do the flowers fail to bloom. Am I not as important as they? "Consider the lilies of the field, they toil not neither do they spin, yet . . . Solomon in all his glory was not arrayed as one of these."

I look at the lavish wastefulness of Nature and know that God intended me to be as abundantly supplied, with everything that makes for beauty, well-being, progressive living and happiness. I, myself, am to blame when these "fruits of the Spirit" fail to appear.

Since I know the Truth of my being, I will no longer hinder or retard my good from coming to me. I will expect and accept all that

I need to make life happy and worth while; for I am a child of the Spirit, and every attribute of It—every attribute of Good—is my inheritance.

Nothing but lack of faith can keep my good from me, for I am one with the Universal Essence of Life, or Spirit, and Its Substance will manifest in my experience *as I believe.* No longer will I go for my good, carrying only a dipper to be filled. This day, as I turn to the Father within, I bring "all the empty vessels" knowing they will be filled, and my abundance will become manifest.

*Abundance Is My Inheritance*

## MY VIBRATION ATTRACTS FRIENDS TO ME

I am never alone, never lonely, for I have as companions and friends those people who are drawn to me by the ever-active and immutable Law of Attraction. I *desire* to be loved, therefore, I allow myself to love greatly, to feel warmly inclined toward people; to be interested in them and helpful on their behalf. I give as I wish to receive. It is not enough that I *profess* to love people. I must really love people, more dearly than I have ever loved before, because all men are my brothers.

I do not outline who shall be my friends and companions, for there is no desire to coerce, compel or suggest to anyone. The Law of Attraction brings into contact and relationship with me all those people in whose company I find the greatest profit and enjoyment and to whom I may give the most.

I am happy and radiant, for I enjoy at all times perfect companionship. I trust implicity the Law of Attraction to bring into my environment and atmosphere friends and loved ones, and establish for me a community of interest and helpfulness. As I love and cooperate with my fellowman, so does he love me and give his cooperation to me. I am happy in all of my companionships and relationships, because they are worked out perfectly by the Law, and the Law is motivated to work for me BY MY LOVE FOR PEOPLE.

*My Loving Thought of Others Attracts Friends to Me*


# PEACE IS THE POWER
# AT THE HEART OF GOD

My peace is found at the heart of God. The heart of God, for me, is found at the very center of my being. It does not matter how closely the confusion of the outer world presses against me, I am not even disturbed by the confusion in my immediate environment. I know that the only way to counteract confusion is to bring peace into play. "Peace I leave with you, my peace I give unto you; not as the world giveth, give I unto you." These words of assurance stay with me, and I hear them re-echoing in the depths of my being.

I surrender all of my fears—those nameless fears which have beset me for such a long time, dulling my pleasure and clouding with misery and apprehension all of my days. I am now through with fear. What, indeed, is there for a divine and immortal being to fear. Certainly *not people*, for as I am a divine and immortal being, so is every man, and every man is my brother. I recognize the one Life Principle, working in and through and inspiring the motives of everyone I contact.

I do not fear sickness, disease or death, because the eternal and perfect Life animates my body and goes always about Its perfect work, healing and renewing that body. I am not afraid of want or lack, for the one infinite Essence supplies me with everything I need all of the time. There is nothing for me to fear, for I am an inseparable part of God. I live in Him; He lives in me; and I draw upon His perfect peace.

*My Peace Is Found at the Heart of God*

## GOD RESTORES ME TO PERFECT HEALTH

The Spirit within me is God, that Spirit is perfect. That Spirit is divine, whole, happy, complete. Spirit of Infinite Peace is within me, and that Peace—poised in perfect life, complete in perfect happiness—that Spirit within me is God and is Whole. That Wholeness is perfect now.

God is an immediate Presence and an immediate Experience in my mind and soul, and I am conscious of this Perfect Presence, this

Divine Wisdom, this Eternal Wholeness. Now I recognize that the Principle of Life is in me and around me and operates through me; that It has no want, has no fear, has no doubt, has no limitation. There is that within me which guides me into opulence, into success, into harmony and love and beauty and friendship, and It does this in peace, in joy and in certainty. I *let* that Divine within me—using whatever method It may—restore me to perfect health, perfect happiness and harmony and bring into my experience everything that is good, that is perfect, that is true and successful.

I am not only *one* with this Spirit, *but this Spirit is all that I am.* It is my whole being, and this Divine Wisdom is in my thought, causing me to act and move intelligently, to make right choices and to follow right pursuits. There are no problems in this Divine Wisdom. Therefore, the road is made straight before me; every obstacle is removed and I am led—irresistibly led—to the Absolute, certain goal of Good, of accomplishment, of success.

*God Restores Me to Perfect Health*


# I ALLOW MYSELF TO DIP DEEPLY INTO MY DIVINE NATURE

This meditation is built from the idea that each one of us has within himself a deeper nature, and, of course, this deeper nature, being an eternal unity with God, or with the Living Spirit, is more than man; it is where the being of man, or the nature of man, merges into the Being of God. So, as we dip deeply into our Divine Natures, let us realize that entering the Secret Presence of this Tabernacle of God, we will, like the Pilgrims of old, have to shed that which does not belong to the Kingdom of Good. We have to deliberately drop that which would hurt. We cannot enter this Gate of Good with a sword in our hands.

So we let go of everything and turn to that Divine Depth within our own nature, wherein the Spirit of God—the Spirit of Love and the Spirit of Peace—dwells with calm serenity. We withdraw into that place within us which has never been hurt, nor has ever been sick, has always and forever lived in divine and eternal peace . . . the Kingdom of God, which is Good. And this Inner Kingdom within is all-peace, all-power and all-perfection. We drop all hate, all fear, all animosity, all resentment. We cast out of our consciousness every doubt and every sense of uncertainty. We know that we are entering into that atmosphere of Wholeness, of happiness and completion where there is no fear, no doubt, no uncertainty, no lack, no want. Here is wholeness, perfection, peace, power, beauty, love, supply and life. We know that the abundance of this life is showered upon us; that we are guided and guarded into right action, into right decision; daily, hourly, minutely, the Principle of Intelligence directs us, the Presence of Love warms us, the Peace of God covers us. And we are led into the pathway of this peace, into the knowledge of this perfection.

We are conscious of the Indwelling God, and we are conscious that the Indwelling God is filling (instantly renewing) our bodies, absolutely eliminating from us whatever there is that does not belong; co-ordinating every function, every organ, every action and reaction (the circulation, the assimilation, the elimination), making it perfect. The Life Principle of every part of our being is perfect and harmonious and now functions perfectly in us. The whole order of discord is changed into the natural order of harmony and wholeness, and we *let* that Divine Power be *exactly what It is* in us. We are no longer afraid, for love casts out fear. Our faith destroys all fear. We awake from the dream of fear to the vision of Reality, where there is no shadow of which to be afraid. We awake from the dream of lack and want and unhappiness to the knowledge of harmony, of abundance and of peace.

*I Allow Myself to Dip Deeply into My Divine Nature*

# PERFECT INTELLIGENCE DIRECTS MY THOUGHT

We now let go of everything and enter into a state of peace. We know the Spirit within us is God, the Living Spirit Almighty . . . that God Who is Infinite, Perfect and Complete, never needed anything, never had any trouble, *never could* destroy; the God Who never operated against Himself, Who never condemned Himself—the Spirit that fashions each of us from His own perfect Being. "All in all, we know Thee, God, omnipresent, full and free; one with every pathway trod, our immortal destiny."

That Infinite Wholeness is perfect peace within us. That Infinite Intelligence is working through us and our affairs; our thought is inspired, guided, governed and directed by Divine Wisdom. That Infinite Wholeness is the circulation of ideas, of intelligence, wisdom, truth and life. It is the elimination of every conception of confusion. It is the assimilation of that which is whole, happy, perfect. The Divine Intelligence is the government of our affairs. Each has within himself this guide to truth, to reason, to beauty, to right action, to certainty and to peace.

*Perfect Intelligence Directs My Thought*

# I AM NOT BOUND BY ANY MISTAKE

Let us now let go of everything and enter into the consciousness of that which we believe. The Spirit within each one of us is God, and It is perfect, It is love, reason, life, truth and beauty. It is limitless and perfect and complete and whole. It knows no lack and no limitation.

There is nothing we have done, said or thought which rises up against us, which has power over us or which limits us; there is no memory of fear, no condemnation for previous mistakes. With the desire to free ourselves from the further indulgence in the mistake, the effect of the previous mistake is wiped out, just as light dissipates the darkness. The Universe holds nothing against us; It can hold nothing against us, because It can know nothing unlike

Itself. Therefore, It only knows us as Perfection. There has never been an occurrence for which we have to suffer! Consequently, every apparent shortcoming—which could be traced to some mental or spiritual infringement of the Law—is not only removed *but the effect is healed!*

That means there is no history to our case. All of its history is this minute wiped out in the knowledge that today the perfect Law—the Law of Freedom—is the only Law there is in our experience. We enter into that freedom with joy, free from every sense of sadness and burden. We enter into it with laughter, with lightness. It is something which lifts us above the heaviness of morbidity and lack and limitation, into that rarer atmosphere where our opinions do not collide, and we enter into it with peace, free from fear.

We know that Infinite Wholeness is in us and through us and around us now, and we are conscious that we are renewed this moment, instantly and perfectly, after the image of Perfection. We are today guided into right action in every exercise of our affairs. Since there is no great and no small to the Infinite, all that seems of little consequence in our lives has the Divine Guidance just as perfectly and completely as that which we think of as being tremendously important. We are guided into the knowledge of happiness, of certainty, of wholeness and of freedom; and we know that there is that subtle Essence of the Spirit, which emanates from us at all times, healing everything It contacts.

*I Am Not Bound by Any Mistake*

# MY IDEAL MERGES INTO THE REAL

We now let go of everything and enter into the contemplation of peace and good and truth and beauty. We are conscious that God is All there is, there is nothing else. We are certain that the Spirit of Reality is our spirit, flows into our spirit and through our spirit. And we are conscious that Love does guide and direct, lead, maintain and sustain. We know that each one of us is a center of this Divine Life, in this Perfect Peace, this Complete Happiness, and this Absolute Wholeness; and we know that this Perfection—which is the center of our very being—is projected into every atom of our being.

We know that the Law of this Being is perfect and there is no obstruction to Its operation. We know that the Principle within us guides us, not only into the way of Truth, but in the way and the performance of that knowledge. WHATEVER IS FOR OUR BENEFIT IS ALREADY PROVIDED. It is all one thing. It is all One Presence, operating through One fundamental Law, therefore, everything necessary to our well-being (whether we think of it as spiritual, mental or physical), everything necessary to remove any belief in obstruction and the inflow and out-push of that Spirit, is brought into our experience. All good, all substance, all supply, all activity, all opportunity for self-expression is ours now!

*My Ideal Merges into the Real*

# I REPRESENT THE PRINCIPLE
# OF PERFECTION

In each human being, the Whole is represented, and the entire knowledge of wisdom, of health, and the perfection of every act, manifests—is represented—and it is through this Inner Divine Voice, the Divine Nature within us, that we are able to perceive and trust, and come into conscious contact with, this Divine Principle. In the sight of this Within, we are perfect. We must try to see ourselves as God sees us, free and filled with vitality and sufficiency for every occasion.

It is not enough to confess that God is the only Power there is. It is only when this consciousness of power is hooked to the dynamo of the mind that there is generated, through the imagination, an embodiment of that which is able to loose it in any direction it sees fit. It is not enough merely to say that there is One Mind and that Mind is God. To this we must add: "That Mind is my mind now." That completes the thought, makes possible a loosing of the Divine Intelligence through our own imagination.

Let us not forget that, in treatment, we must sense the embodiment of that which we wish to experience. The statements which are made in the treatment are for the purpose of delivering to the imagination, in a certain form, THAT WHICH WAS TRUE BEFORE WE MADE THE STATEMENTS. The whole problem is not one of *creation*, but one of *direction*, and there is no direction unless there is first an embodiment. Let us try this in our meditation. We know that we reflect the Divine Perfection and that there is an intuition within us which guides us. We know that all the power there is and all the presence there is, is this perfect Spirit, this Divine Reality, which is around us and through us and in us. Now, each turning directly to his own thought, says:

"The Spirit within me, which is God, the Living Spirit Almighty, is Perfection. It is Wholeness; It is Peace. It is Divine Guidance, Perfect Peace, Complete Wholeness, Absolute Perfection, and right now, this moment, this Spirit governs every act of my life. It surrounds me with Light, in which there is no darkness, no gloom, no heaviness and no fear. In this Light, I live and move and have my being. And this Light dispels all darkness and casts out all fear.

"This Divine Wisdom within me guides every act, directs everything in my life, toward happiness, toward peace, toward power; and being the Spirit of Love, It surrounds me with beauty, with friendship and with joy. Being the Giver of Life, every day I receive that which is perfect, abundant, happy, joyful and free. Being that Divine Thing which individualizes in me, It is entirely individual, personal and unique. I am the expression of my own complete self, and there is no barrier or bar to that self-expression. Being the Spirit of Substance, that Spirit within me is the Father of Supply, and It brings to me everything necessary to my unfoldment, and keeps me in the wisdom through which It governs me, now and forever."

*I Represent the Principle of Perfection*

# I TAKE THE CHRIST WAY TO FULFILLMENT

When Jesus said, "No man cometh unto the Father but by me," of course, he meant the I AM. This I AM, then, means the inner Reality of every man's nature, and when we stop to figure it out, how can we come unto God, the Living Spirit, except through the avenues of our own consciousness, which is the only approach to God we could possibly have? It is another way of saying that the only way we shall ever approach Reality is by uncovering the Divinity already latent within our own consciousness, in our own soul, in the center of our own being.

Every man is Divine and the *Christ Way* is the way of the unfoldment of his Divinity through his humanity; the uncovering of his spiritual individuality and the use that his personal man, or his personality, makes of it. Meditation is for the purpose of consciously recognizing man's Divinity and uncovering it. In order to come into the Christ Way, into the consciousness of our own Divinity, we lay aside every fear or doubt or worry, and we enter into the silent, peaceful contemplation that the Spirit of the Living God is within us—all the Power there is, all the Presence there is, and all the Life there is, is right here. Each one turns to himself, knowing that:

"The Spirit within me is God, that Spirit is perfect, and because that Spirit is perfect, my knowledge of that Spirit destroys every doubt, every fear, casts out all uncertainty and all unbelief, and fills me with a knowledge of my own perfection. There is that within me which is perfect, Divine, happy and whole and harmonious. There is that within me that has never been afraid, never been limited, and it is this Christ Nature within me that I now recognize and speak into manifestation through my being; that the Spirit within me, which is perfect, shall remove every consciousness of disease, shall stimulate activity and recognize perfect circulation of these Divine ideas, and establish within me, not only the knowledge of that Divine Perfection which I really am, but shall establish in my physical being a manifestation of that knowledge of Reality, or the realization of that Presence, and whatever there might be within me, which does not belong, is now eliminated, cast out and destroyed.

"Divine Guidance IS, and that Perfect Intelligence is now governing the activity of my life into the fulfillment of joy, into the fulfillment of love, of unity, of happiness and success, now and at all times."

*I Take the Christ Way to Fulfillment*

## THE ETERNAL CYCLES OF LIFE IN MOTION FULFILL MY FAITH

This is another way of saying that something happens when a man believes. Faith is operated upon by some principle which is a government of Law and Order, and which has within Itself the power to execute Itself. Prayer is not to ask God to be God. There is a Supreme Intelligence in the Universe, we cannot tell It anything; what little we know, we have drawn from It. There is an Absolute Spirit around us, It does not need our existence. It has already surrendered Itself to us but we have not yet surrendered ourselves to It. That is what prayer—or treatment—is for. We do not pray the Principle of Peace to desist from confusion, but we seek that Peace that it shall enter into our confused souls. Therefore, prayer or meditation is for the purpose of becoming receptive to the Divine Influx, which already owns everything, knows everything, governs all things, and creates what we need—if we but permit it to—in Its own Nature, which is goodness, truth and beauty. Each turns to the within in something after this fashion:

We let go of everything, drop every fear from our minds, drop all confusion from our thought, and enter into the inner secret communion with that great Reality, which is our Universal Self—God— in Whom we live and move and have our being. We are conscious that this Divine Presence overshadows and indwells. It is both *without* this physical, mental being and *within* this physical, mental being. Therefore, It is the spiritual Reality of this being, the I AM, which is Universal, Eternal and Perfect.

Now this Spirit is our Spirit. It is our life from which we now draw full, complete and perfect being. This Divine Intelligence does govern us intelligently; It does direct us consciously, accurately, unerringly. We surrender to It every fear, every sense of uncertainty of the future, every thought of any morbidity of the past. We surrender all confusion and doubt, and we know that this Divine Influx removes every mental obstruction to peace; It removes every sense of condemnation and judgment, and we enter into the fulfillment of Its perfection now. We believe if there is any part of our physical being which needs healing, It heals it; that that Power within us and around us which creates, can re-create, can make whole now. We believe if there is any conflict in our mental being, it can be removed, because the Spirit is higher than the mind and more than the body, and we are dealing with that Spirit which, animating the mind with Divine Intelligence, produces an influx of spiritual life in the body, healing, without effort, both mind and body. We relinquish, we let go, those things which bother us mentally or hurt us physically. We know that the Divine Presence is the Eternal Healer, because It is the everlasting Giver of life. And we know the Intelligence which created the Universe and projected it in form and governs it with perfect Law—that Divine Being directs our movements intelligently, coherently, constructively, certainly, bringing to each that which he calls success and prosperity, happiness, fulfillment of life, action. And we know that that Divine Being, governing everything out of Its own Nature, works without effort—Birthless and Deathless and Tireless, It moves through us to perfect ends, now.

*The Eternal Cycles of Life in Motion Fulfill My Faith*

# About the Author

Ernest Holmes (1887–1960) was an internationally recognized authority on religious psychology and the founder of the Religious Science movement. There are currently hundreds of churches and spiritual centers across the country that are based on his teaching, and three international organizations dedicated to his philosophy: United Church of Religious Science, Religious Science International, and Associated New Thought Network. Holmes's writings and philosophy have influenced countless teachers and authors, and have inspired millions. His beloved books include the seminal text *The Science of Mind, This Thing Called You, Creative Mind, Creative Mind and Success, The Art of Life* (previously published as *This Thing Called Life*), *Love and Law, Prayer, The Hidden Power of the Bible, The Essential Ernest Holmes,* and *365 Science of Mind.*

You can find more information about Holmes and his teachings at www.scienceofmind.com.

# DISCOVER THE WORLD
# OF ERNEST HOLMES

## *The Landmark Guide to Spiritual Living*

*The Science of Mind: The Definitive Edition*

*A Philosophy, a Faith, a Way of Life*

978-0-87477-865-6 (hardcover)

978-0-87477-921-9 (paperback)

## *Simple Guides for Ideas in Action*

*Creative Mind* 978-1-58542-606-5 • *The Art of Life* 978-1-58542-613-3

*Creative Mind and Success* 978-1-58542-608-9

*This Thing Called You* 978-1-58542-607-2

*"There is a power for good in this Universe greater than you, and you can use it."*

—ERNEST HOLMES

## A Treasury of Inspiration and Guidance

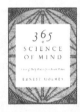

365 Science of Mind

978-1-58542-609-6

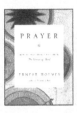

Prayer

978-1-58542-605-8

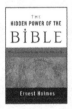

The Hidden Power
of the Bible

978-1-58542-511-2

Love and Law:
The Unpublished
Teachings

978-1-58542-302-6

The Essential
Ernest Holmes

978-1-58542-181-7

TARCHER
PENGUIN

www.penguin.com

www.scienceofmind.com